F
i
Pennsylvania

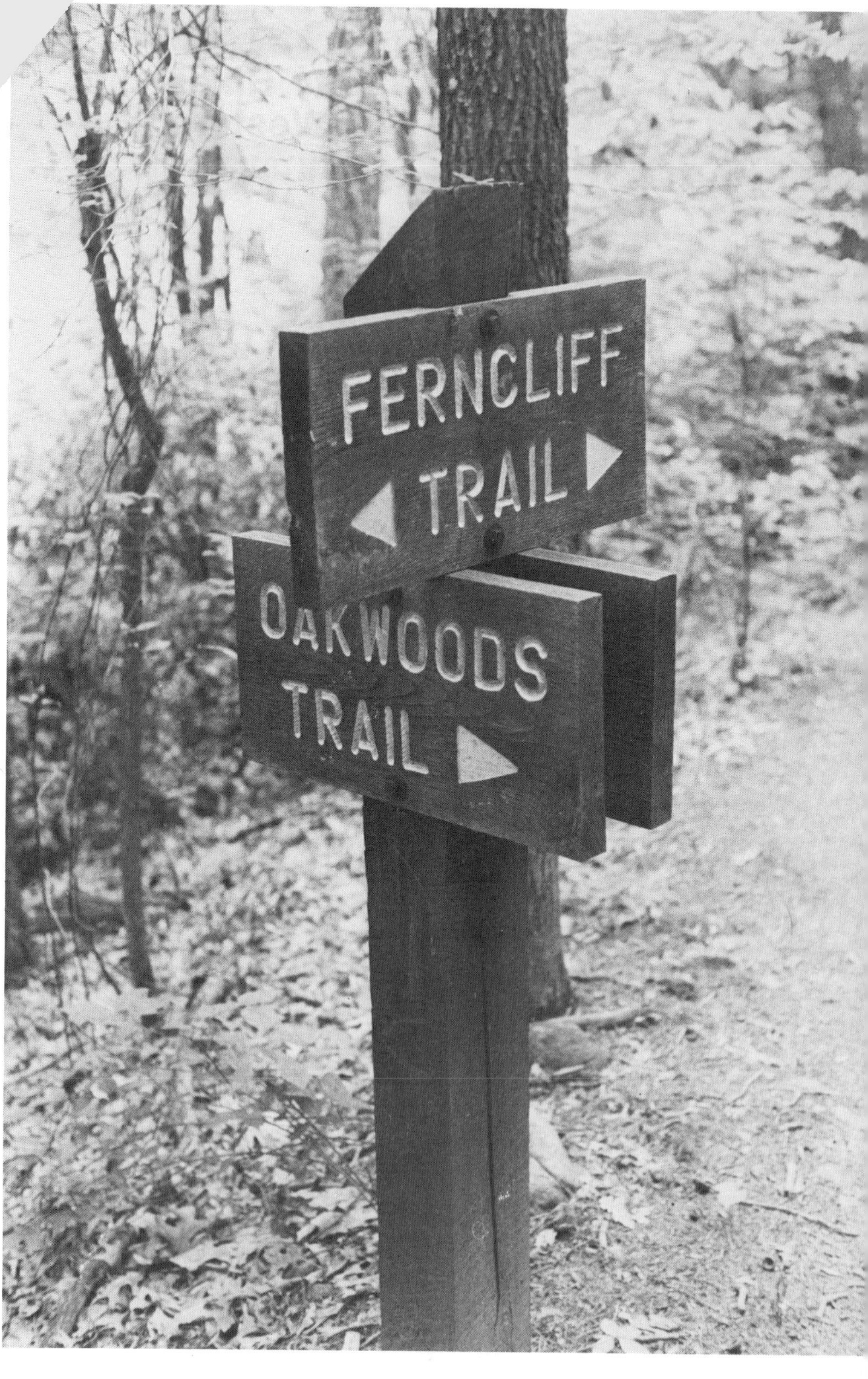

FERNCLIFF
TRAIL
OAKWOODS
TRAIL

Fifty Hikes in Western Pennsylvania

Walks and Day Hikes
From the Laurel Highlands
to Lake Erie

Second Edition

Tom Thwaites

Photographs by the Author

Backcountry
Publications
Woodstock, Vt.

An Invitation to the Reader

Housing developments, logging, mining, fires—these and other works of man and nature take their toll on hiking trails. If you find that conditions along any of these 50 hikes have changed, please let the author and publisher know so that they may correct future editions. Address correspondence to:

Editor
Fifty Hikes™ Series
Backcountry Publications
PO Box 748
Woodstock, VT 05091

Acknowledgements

This book could not have been written without the help of many hikers living in western Pennsylvania. Among those who suggested hikes, served as hiking companions and provided trailhead services, car shuttles, shelter, food and information were Mary Ann and Steve McGuire, Glenn Oster, Bill Dzombak, Ray Gerard, Ruth and Norm Samuelson, Dave Gregg, Mark Place, Paul Wiegman, Jerry Bosiljevac, Bob Peppel, Mitch Dickerson, Hugh Downing, Roger Cuffey, Dave Maxwell, Wanda Harp, Janeal Hedman, and Mark Eckler. I am particularly grateful to my wife, Barbara, who typed the manuscript. I also thank my editor, John Pierson, for his help and patience.

Library of Congress Cataloging-in Publication Data

Thwaites, Tom.
    Fifty hikes in western Pennsylvania: walks and day hikes from the Laurel Highlands to Lake Erie/Tom Thwaites; photographs by the author. — 2nd ed.
        p. cm.
    Includes bibliographical references.
    ISBN 0-88150-163-8
    1. Hiking—Pennsylvania—Guide-books. 2. Pennsylvania-
-Description and travel—1981- —Guide-books. I. Title.
II. Title: 50 hikes in western Pennsylvania.
GV199.42.P4T49   1990
796.5′1′09748—dc20   90-33327
                                                                          CIP

Published by Backcountry Publications, a division of
   The Countryman Press, PO Box 748, Woodstock, VT 05091
Distributed by W.W. Norton & Company, Inc., 500 Fifth Avenue,
   New York, NY 10110
Text design by Wladislaw Finne
Cover photo of the Allegheny Forest taken by Jim Baron, Image Finders
Paste-up by Leslie Fry
Trail maps by Richard Widhu

To my wife,
Barbara

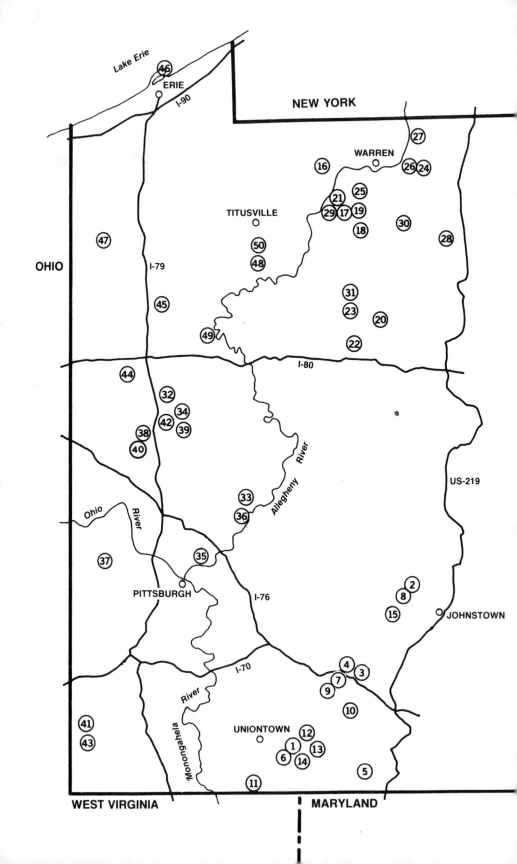

Contents

Erie and the North   183

Introduction

Hiking Trails in western Pennsylvania are less rugged than those in the central and eastern parts of the state. This happy condition is a consequence of geology.

Today, western Pennsylvania is a plateau cut through by many river valleys. It was not always so. When the rocks in this part of the state were laid down in the Paleozoic Era, hundreds of millions of years ago, Pennsylvania was south of the equator and frequently under water. To the east there were high mountains, which probably resembled the Cordillera Blanco of Peru. Material eroded from these mountains was carried west to the shallow sea that covered much of North America. Hudson's Bay may be a relic of this ancient sea.

When this sea was fairly deep, limestones were deposited. When it was shallow, mud collected and shales were formed. When the sea retreated altogether, sandstones were laid down. Crossbedding of these sandstones indicates that they were deposited by streams which flowed across vast deltas that stretched from the mountains to what remained of the sea.

Later in the Paleozoic, swampy forests of tree ferns grew on these deltas and eventually became the coal seams of western Pennsylvania. Coal is only one of many energy resources in Penn's Woods. In 1859, the world's first oil well was drilled near Titusville. More than a century later, as you will see on several hikes, oil and gas wells are still being drilled.

After this great layer cake of rock had been formed, our continent collided with North Africa, forming the super continent Pangaea. Mountains were produced that probably resembled the Himalayas. The roots of these folded mountains, much eroded, form the ridge-and-valley region of central and eastern Pennsylvania. The folds reached into western Pennsylvania but were much gentler. By the time North America split from Pangaea, these mountains had been eroded to a flat plain.

For reasons that are still obscure, the Appalachians were again uplifted, forming the plateau we see today. The anticlines of Negro Mountain, Laurel Hill and Chestnut Ridge were re-excavated by erosion and their tops form the highest elevations in Penn's Woods.

The rivers draining this plateau cut deep valleys into it. Most of them, including the Youghiogheny and the Allegheny, flowed northwest into the Saint Lawrence River where Lake Erie is today. The Ice Age changed this simple pattern. Glacier after glacier profoundly altered the northwestern part of the state, dotting the area with lakes, swamps and bogs and changing the course of rivers well beyond the reach of the ice. Some rivers were buried by glacial debris, and it is impossible to trace their preglacial routes. Other rivers had to reverse their flow. The Allegheny and Ohio rivers of today contain sections where water flows "uphill."

These great events formed the earth's crust into the setting for the hikes in this book. Rock layers on the western plateau are nearly horizontal, and even the anticlines have only a modest slope. In the ridge-and-valley region to the east, many rock layers stand on edge and have been shattered by erosion into enormous rock piles. For hikers the result is that slopes are gentler and trails less rocky in western Pennsylvania than in the central and eastern parts of the Commonwealth.

Hikers are generally restricted to public lands, and public lands are relatively scarce in western Pennsylvania. With roughly 200,000 hectares (494,000 acres), the Allegheny National Forest forms the largest tract of public land west of US 219. Next are some 100,000 hectares (247,000 acres) of state game lands. Although organized trails are scarce, the game lands are widely distributed. One is even found just outside Pittsburgh. Hiking trails are also found in state forests, state and county parks and lands belonging to the Western Pennsylvania Conservancy. Many of the best hiking areas in western Pennsylvania— including large parts of Ohiopyle, McConnells Mill, Moraine, Oil Creek and Laurel Ridge state parks, as well as Forbes State Forest and Jennings Nature Reserve—were purchased by the Western Pennsylvania Conservancy and transferred to public ownership. Sometimes it seems that a hiker would not be able legally to step off a road in western Pennsylvania were it not for the Conservancy.

As regards insects, Pennsylvania's location is a happy one. It is just far enough south to escape the black flies and just far enough north to avoid most of the ticks, at least the big dog ticks. But there are gnats that, while a distant second to black flies, nevertheless, try harder. Mosquitoes are abundant in the swampy areas. Deer flies can be a real nuisance as they try to carve off a steak.

Spring wildflowers are a particular delight of western Pennsylvania trails. Since the western part of the state is drier than the central part, this bounty must come from richer soils. The growing season is comprised of a few short weeks between the melting of the snows and the leafing of the trees. Wildflowers are not distributed uniformly along the trails: in some places there are hardly any, while in others they cover the ground like a late snowfall.

Hiking has much to recommend it as a recreational activity. It offers the cardiovascular advantages of jogging and bicycling, but with much less damage to the knees, ankles and feet than jogging and virtually no exposure to dangerous traffic. A jogger at age forty may have the best cardiovascular system of anyone using a wheelchair. Bicycling is still recreation, but as the supply of petroleum dwindles and synthetic fuel prices rise, bicycling will become serious transportation. Hiking will continue to be recreational.

There are other benefits from hiking. Hiking brings us closer to nature and our roots in the natural world. Hiking reminds us that food does not come from the supermarket, wood does not come from the lumber yard and water does not come from the faucet. Hikers share the delights and dilemmas of those who cannot live without things that are natural, wild and free.

There are emotional benefits from hiking, too. John Muir wrote: "Climb the mountains and get their good tidings. Nature's peace will flow into you as sunshine flows into trees. The winds will blow their own freshness into you, and the storms their energy, while cares will drop off like autumn leaves."

George W. Sears (1821-1890) was Pennsylvania's pioneer conservationist and outdoor writer. "Nessmuk," as Sears was called, put it this way: "We do not go to the . . . woods to rough it, we go

Ohiopyle Falls

to smooth it. We get it rough enough . . . in towns and cities."

It's true! Whenever pressures and problems drive me to the woods, the miracle works again. A few hours of hiking, a view of the countryside, a long drink from a spring, and I can feel my problems drop away or shrink into perspective. I am freshly astonished.

About This Book

Detailed instructions are given here for fifty hikes on public lands or private lands where hiking is permitted. Since western Pennsylvania trails are, with few exceptions, poorly measured, all the hikes in this book were measured with a Rolatape measuring wheel of two meter circumference. The distance given for each hike is how far you will walk to complete the hike as described. Where hikes can be shortened, instructions are included.

The hiking times were determined by my SMAP (Standard Middle-Aged Pace). Those who have just taken up hiking may find their times exceed mine. Young hikers in good condition will have no trouble shortening them. But keep in mind that hiking is not a race and that it is the quality of the experience that counts.

The rise listed for each hike is the total amount of climbing obtained by adding together all the ups in an up-and-down hike. In some car shuttle hikes— such as Maple Summit to Ohiopyle and Hemlock Run—the rise would be greatly increased if the hike were done in the opposite direction. In all cases the rise has been determined from the USGS 7 1/2' topographic maps.

There are 15 short or introductory hikes in this book. They range up to 8 kilometers (5 miles) long and up to three hours hiking time. Novice hikers should

try one or more of these short hikes before moving up to day hikes. Twenty-eight hikes range from 8 kilometers (5 miles) to 16 kilometers (10 miles) and are classed as day hikes. Some of these could be turned into two-day backpacks, providing you can arrange to be dropped off and picked up and don't have to leave your car overnight at a trailhead. Cars left overnight may be drained of gas, ransacked or vandalized. In the Allegheny National Forest, check with the Allegheny Outdoor Club (see end of introduction for address) or the Chapman State Park Office (R.D., Box 1610, Clarendon, PA 16313, tel. (814) 723-5030). They may be able to help you arrange trailhead service. Or consult Keystone Trail Association's Trailhead Transportation Guide, which lists public transportation to trails and state parks (P.O. Box 251, Cogan Station, PA 17728). Plans call for updating this guide every year, so make sure you have the most recent edition.

Finally, there are seven "bootbuster" hikes ranging from 16 kilometers (10 miles) to 20.6 kilometers (12.8 miles). These are challenges for the most seasoned hikers. Again, some of them could be turned into backpacks.

Maps are listed in each description. United States Geological Survey (USGS) maps are always listed but usually do not show the actual trails. State park maps are better for trails but do not show contours. What's more, state maps tend to be optimistic, sometimes showing trails that are no longer maintained or that may never have been cut. The best trail maps are those prepared by the organization responsible for trail maintenance. Copies of the Pennsylvania Recreation Guide and Highway map, which lists state parks and their facilities and activities, are available from the Office of Public Information of the

Department of Environmental Resources. For information on where to order maps, see the list of addresses at the end of the introduction.

The fifty hikes are grouped into four geographic areas. Thirty-one hikes are concentrated in the Laurel Highlands and Allegheny National Forest areas. The remainder are in the Pittsburgh or Lake Erie areas, which are divided by I-80.

Equipment and Clothing

Hiking clothes should be comfortable. They do not have to be new or fashionable or expensive. In summer, when the primary task is keeping cool, hiking shorts and short-sleeved shirts are appropriate, but to protect yourself from ticks, which may carry Lyme disease, you will want long pants and long-sleeved shirts. You're going to sweat a lot more come summer. The only equipment required is a day pack for carrying your canteen, insect repellent and rain gear if the weather looks threatening. Don't try to cram these items into your pockets.

Canteens are made of metal or plastic. If you leave some space for expansion, you can freeze the water in a plastic canteen in the freezer overnight and so provide yourself with a supply of ice water on the trail. The only advantage of a metal canteen is that you can put it directly on a stove in winter to thaw the ice trying to form inside.

In fall and spring, the demands on clothing escalate. Temperatures may vary from near freezing in the morning to warm on a sunny afternoon. Also, the weather can turn hypothermic with little or no warning. These are the seasons when you appreciate wool and polypropylene clothing. You may need one of the larger day packs to carry the layers you will shed as the day warms up, in addition to the items already mentioned.

Winter conditions are highly variable across western Pennsylvania. Snow depths may reach a meter or more in the Alleghenys and on Laurel Ridge, while other places may be bare. Deep snow requires snowshoes or cross-country skis; trying to hike without them leads quickly to exhaustion. Hypothermia is even more of a threat in winter. It can rain in winter, too. Yet there is as much beauty in the woods in this season as in the others.

Backpacking requires a lot more equipment than day hiking. You will need a sleeping bag, a backpack and some kind of shelter. Since you will spend about one-third of your time in the sleeping bag, it's important to get one that's really comfortable. Mummy bags are much warmer than the traditional rectangular bags, but some people find mummy bags too confining. A bewildering variety of designs and materials is available, including some compromises between rectangular and mummy bags. For Appalachia's temperate rain forest, synthetic fillings such as Polarguard and Holofill are your best bets. They are slightly heavier than down, but are cheaper and will keep you warm even if they get wet. Line the stuff sack with a plastic bag to make sure your sleeping bag stays dry.

A good backpack is basically a collection of pockets of various sizes. The internal frame packs so popular today are designed for cross-country skiing and mountain climbing. For general purpose backpacking, the external frame pack is still the best. Backpacks should be fitted to your height. If a store wants to sell you a backpack without trying it on, take your business elsewhere. A padded hipbelt allows you to transfer 50 to 90 percent of the pack's weight directly to your hips, bypassing all those fragile discs in your back.

Adirondack-type shelters are available only on the Laurel Highlands Trail. These shelters have an open front, a good roof and a fireplace. Elsewhere in western Pennsylvania, you will have to carry your own shelter. A waterproof nylon tarp is the lightest and cheapest solution. However, when bugs are really bad, you will need a tent with good ventilation. Again, a variety of designs is available. The best advice is to rent before you buy.

An item of equipment that can greatly reduce your mark on the landscape is a backpacking stove. It leaves no pile of charcoal at your campsite and poses a minimal fire hazard. A variety of designs and fuels is available, and you should try several before investing in your own. When buying hiking and backpacking equipment, beware of large retail chains. Seek out an outing store where the clerks know what they are selling.

Footwear

The most important and specialized part of a hiker's equipment is footwear. Shoes or boots for hiking must have good arch support and should also protect your feet from impacts with rocks, roots, sticks and logs. Ideally, your footwear should also keep your feet dry in rain, snow or wet brush. Besides being cold and uncomfortable, wet feet develop blisters far faster than dry ones.

Leather hiking boots with lugged soles are almost ideal. Lugged soles look like a flexible waffle iron. These boots are available at outing stores, but they have been priced into hyperspace. Many hikers must search for cheaper alternatives and make a variety of compromises.

Walking shoes are low cut with leather uppers and some kind of rubber (even lugged) sole. Walking shoes must have good arch support. Usually they can pass for street shoes and are frequently worn as such. They do not provide any ankle support and are suitable only for day hiking on good trails. Since they are low cut, it doesn't matter whether they are waterproof; rain and snow have plenty of access anyway. Walking shoes are available at a wide range of prices, up to what real hiking boots cost just a few years ago. Old running shoes frequently see service as walking shoes, but their flexible soles let you feel every root and rock.

Another alternative is the ankle-high work boot. These were the traditional footgear of hikers before the European hiking boot arrived. Since they are generally made of split leather, they are difficult to waterproof. Work boots are available at a range of prices and with a variety of soles, including lugged. They are adequate for backpacking on good trails, but do not provide as much ankle support as real hiking boots.

A third and more expensive alternative is the lightweight Gore-Tex hiking boot. I've never worn them, but those who have used them claim they can really bounce along the trails. Others says Gore-Tex boots aren't always waterproof.

Wait until you are sure the hiking bug has bitten before investing in a pair of real hiking boots. When and if you do, be sure to get boots of full grain leather with as few seams as possible. With good care, they should carry you along the trail for years to come.

The worst thing that can happen to leather shoes or boots is to get them soaked. Drying must be done slowly at room temperature. Even a few such wettings will greatly reduce the life of a leather boot. Purchase large enough boots so that you can wear at least two pairs of socks—a thin inner sock of polypropylene and a thick, mostly wool, outer sock—without cramping your feet.

Safety in the Woods

Compared with our roads and highways the woods are relatively safe. Once you've parked your car and gotten a few strong trees between you and the nearest road, the chances of your being injured or killed have dropped.

Don't worry about the snakes. They are rare and belong on the endangered species list in Pennsylvania. Besides, they are big enough to see. Just don't pick them up. Today the real threats to your health are microbial. First are giardia and other microbes found in streams, springs and other unprotected water sources. Fill your canteen before you leave home or get your drinking water from tested supplies. On a backpack you will have to use untested sources. Pump it through a submicron filter such as First Need or Katadyn to remove giardia cysts and bacteria.

The other threat is Lyme disease, caused by a corkscrew-shaped bacteria called a spirochete but transmitted to humans by a tiny creature no larger than the period at the end of this sentence. This is the nymph or immature stage of Ixodes dammini, the deer tick. Although the larger mature deer ticks can also transmit the disease, about 80 percent of cases seem to be due to nymphs. Since the nymphs are so small and their bites painless, most people are unaware they have been bitten.

Lyme disease is difficult to diagnose and many physicians don't wait for symptoms to develop but will put anyone who has been bitten by a deer tick on a course of antibiotics. Symptoms of Lyme disease include skin rash, flu, arthritis, stiff neck, chills and fever, extreme fatigue, swollen glands, sore throat, severe headaches, body aches, joint pains and bone pains. If untreated, the arthritis may cause irreversible damage. Neurological and cardiac symptoms can also develop. One of the difficulties in diagnosing Lyme disease is that it resembles so many other diseases. Blood and urine tests for Lyme disease are useful but not completely reliable.

You don't have to go to the woods to get Lyme disease. Many people contract Lyme disease in their own back yards or gardens. Adult deer ticks live and mate on white tailed deer. So if you ever see deer from your windows you are at risk. You don't even have to go outside. Your dog or cat can bring ticks right into your living room. Deer ticks are most active in late spring and summer and can also be active the rest of the year, even on warm days in winter.

There are lots of precautions you can take when hiking to protect yourself against deer ticks and Lyme disease. Wear light-colored long pants, long-sleeved shirts, closed shoes and socks that come up over the bottom edge of your pants. In summer this new fashion will be insufferably hot. Apply insect repellent (DEET) to the outside of your pants, socks and shoes. A new repellent (Permanone) which actually kills ticks has recently been licensed for sale in Pennsylvania, but is not widely available. Check with Coulston International of Easton, PA for a supplier near you.

If you must wear shorts, you'll have to put DEET right on your skin. DEET is absorbed through the skin and is suspected of causing epileptic-type seizures in children. Long-term effects of DEET on adults are not known. When hiking, keep to the middle of the trail and don't lie down or sit in grass or other vegetation. When you get home, inspect yourself for ticks; have somebody else inspect your back. A tick must bite for 10 to 12 hours to transmit Lyme disease. Remove ticks carefully with tweezers, taking care to get the mouth parts out of your skin. Don't handle the tick as the spirochetes could enter through cracks in your skin. Save the tick in a bottle to show to the doctor.

Lyme disease can be treated at all stages with antibiotics; as with other diseases there is a premium on early treatment. If you think you may have been exposed, call the American Lyme Disease Foundation at 1-800-876-LYME for the name of a physician in your area who specializes in treating Lyme Disease.

The number of reported cases of Lyme disease has increased dramatically in recent years, but it is not clear just how much of this increase can be attributed to better diagnosis.

Lyme disease does not compel one to stay home. You can still hike Pennsylvania's beautiful woods if you take a few precautions.

Other dangers to be aware of are the hunters during bear and deer season in late November and early December. Check with a local office of the game commission, a local newspaper or a hunter for the exact dates.

Stinging insects—hornets, wasps and yellow jackets—are another hazard in Penn's Woods. To people allergic to their stings, these insects can be life threatening. Yellow jackets nest underground, even in the middle of trails. You usually don't know you have stepped into a nest until you feel the first fiery sting. Then all you can do is run through some brush, swiping and swatting, to escape the vengeful horde.

Cold, wet weather presents yet another hazard. If you get soaked at any time when the temperature is below 10 degrees Celsius (50 degrees Fahrenheit), you are in trouble. Garments of wool, pile, Polarguard, Holofill, Thinsulate, etc. are your best defense against hypothermia. Even in the initial stages, before uncontrollable shivering sets in, your judgment and perception are dangerously and insidiously impaired. Be alert for signs of hypothermia in your companions. Slurred or incoherent speech, stumbling, falling and violent shivering are all signs of hypothermia. Treatment consists of warming the victim by getting him or her into a shelter and/ or a sleeping bag. Alcoholic beverages will only make things worse.

Another threat from the weather is lightning. Don't stand under a tall tree or in an open field when lightning is around. For once, a car is about the safest place to be.

Lastly, beware of any wild animal that does not flee at your approach. Any animal that acts strangely must be suspected of having rabies. Should you be bitten by any wild animal, including a bat, make every effort to kill it so that its brain can be tested by the veterinary diagnostic laboratory in Harrisburg. Should the animal escape, you will have to undergo the entire series of shots for rabies.

Respect for the Land and Its Inhabitants

Once you step off a road, your environmental impact increases dramatically. It used to be that man felt threatened by nature. But the numbers of our species have reversed this rule. Now it's the land and its wild inhabitants that are vulnerable. Carry out litter in pack or pockets; don't leave it to degrade the landscape. Some of our litter—bottles and aluminum cans—is of geologic permanence. Be careful with fire. Forest fires kill woods and wildlife. Never leave a campfire unattended: make sure it is dead before you move on. Try to build a campfire only where one has been built before. Don't smoke in the woods. Refrain from collecting wild plants or injuring live trees or shrubs.

Although hikers' use of the land constitutes the lightest of human impacts, even it can be overdone. Avoid overused hiking and camping areas.

There are things you can do to improve hiking and backpacking in Penn's Woods. The Appalachian Trail was built largely by volunteers and is maintained exclusively by them. If the projected North Country Trail from New York to North Dakota is ever to be completed, it will be built by volunteers. Join one or more of the organizations listed below, which are involved in building and maintaining hiking trails. A few people with hand tools can work miracles. Physically and emotionally, the rewards of trail work are as real as they are little known.

Hiking Organizations

Keystone Trails Association
P.O. Box 251
Cogan Station, PA 17728
   Updates to the hikes in this book will be given in the "Hiker Alert" column of the *Keystone Trails Association Newsletter*.

Western Pennsylvania Conservancy
316 Fourth Avenue
Pittsburgh, PA 15222

Sierra Club, Allegheny Group
P.O. Box 8241
Pittsburgh, PA 15217

American Youth Hostels
Pittsburgh Council
6300 Fifth Avenue
Pittsburgh, PA 15232

Allegheny Outdoor Club
c/o Brita Dorn
Star Route, Box 476
Sheffield, PA 16346

North Country Trail Association
P.O. Box 311
White Cloud, MI 49349

Other Books

Pennsylvania Hiking Trails. 11th ed. Keystone Trails Association, 1993.
Hiker's Guide to the Laurel Highlands Trail. 4th ed. Sierra Club – Allegheny Group, 1992.
Allegheny National Forest Hiking Guide, 3rd ed. (1990). Sierra Club – Allegheny Group.
Baker Trail Guide. American Youth Hostels-Pittsburgh Council, 1986.

Maps and Where To Get Them

United States Geological Survey Maps:
   Distribution Branch
   U. S. Geological Survey
   Box 25286 Federal Center, Bldg. 41
   Denver, Co 80225 ($4.00 per map)

State park maps:
   From individual state park offices or:
   Bureau of State Parks
   P.O. Box 8551
   Harrisburg, PA 17105-8551
   Phone: 1-800-63 PARKS

Public use maps for state forests:
  From individual state forest offices
  or
  Department of Conservation
  and Natural Resources
  or
  Bureau of Forestry
  P.O. Box 1467
  Harrisburg, PA 17120

State game lands recreation maps:
  Pennsylvania Game Commission
  Dept. AR, 2001 Elmerton Ave.
  Harrisburg, PA 17110
  (50 cents per map)

Visit the Keystone Trails Association
website at
http://www.reston.com/kta/kta.html;
or the Allegheny National Forest at
http://www.penn.com/~anf

U. S. Forest Service maps:
  Allegheny National Forest
  Box 847
  Warren, PA 16356
  ($3.00 charge for Allegheny National
  Forest map)

Key to Map Symbols

——————————— main trail

• • • • • • side trail

P parking

Laurel Highlands

1

Ferncliff Natural Area

Distance: 3.3 km (2.1 miles)
Time: 1½ hours
Rise: 60 meters (200 feet)
Highlight: Ohiopyle Falls
Maps: USGS 7½' Ohiopyle, Fort Necessity; state park map

Ferncliff is a peninsula surrounded on three sides by the Youghiogheny River (pronounced: YAHK-ah-gainy). The river's name, like many others in Pennsylvania, is a white man's corruption of an Indian name. It is a magical area that reminds me of Point Lobos on the California coast. Perhaps it's the roar of the rapids and falls that reminds me of the surf, but it's also the sense of remoteness and isolation. Nearby Ohiopyle village and the rest of the state park seem completely cut off by the violence of the river. Around the Ferncliff Peninsula the Youghiogheny drops 30 meters in just 1.5 km (1 mile), producing Ohiopyle Falls and half a dozen rapids. Another point of resemblance to Point Lobos is the poison ivy that keeps you on the trails.

As with several other natural areas and reserves, Ferncliff Natural Area was originally acquired and operated by the Western Pennsylvania Conservancy.

The peninsula has been formed by the gradual retreat of Ohiopyle Falls. At one time or another, the Youghiogheny may have flowed over the entire peninsula. Pot holes, such as you see at the brink of the falls, are also found above

today's river level. The Youghiogheny River flows from the mountains to the south and brings with it seeds of southern plants. Thus Ferncliff is the northern outpost for many southern plants. Among these is the buffalo nut, a parasitic shrub that grows on the roots of mountain laurel. The Buffalo Nut Trail at Ferncliff is named after this shrub. Walking shoes are fine for this short hike.

The trailhead can be reached only from PA 381. Turn west just north of the bridge over the Yough and before you reach the two tracks of the Baltimore and Ohio Railroad. Bear left at the sign into one of the parking lots. Follow the signs to the trailhead. The Ferncliff Trail is a self-guiding nature trail and is marked with black blazes. These blazes are easier to follow than you might think. The trail takes you under the old Western Maryland Railroad bridge to a trail junction and marker noting that Ferncliff was declared a National Natural Landmark in 1973. Follow the Ferncliff Trail as it bears left to emerge at the water's edge where a line is stretched across the river to keep boats, swimmers and fishermen from going over Ohiopyle Falls. Near 0.3 km (0.2 mile)

Fossil Tree Fern

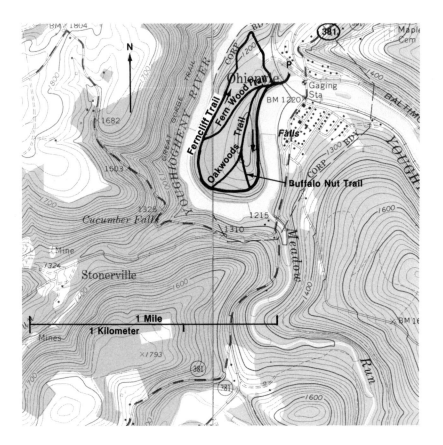

look for a fossil tree fern in the bedrock. It stretches almost entirely across the trail and is probably a lepidodendron or scale tree. Soon you see poison ivy edging the trail mostly on the right. Note driftwood logs lodged high above the normal level of the river. The shore here is bordered with thick jungles of rhododendron. When you reach the brink of the falls, the trail is forced out onto the ledges. Near 0.6 km (0.4 mile) turn left for an overlook of Ohiopyle Falls. The falls are formed by the resistant Pottsville sandstone.

The overlook is from the brink of a cliff and has no guard rails, so watch your step. Perhaps it was from this very spot that George Washington viewed the falls in 1754 while trying to find a way to move men and supplies for the attack on Fort Dusquesne. He may have thought that the reports of the waterfall had been exaggerated; waterfalls never lose much in the reporting process. But George was convinced and gave up the idea of water travel on the Yough. To the right, you can see the put-in place for today's travel on the lower Yough by kayak and raft.

Back on the trail you climb to the top of the cliff, tunneling through the rhododendron between large hemlocks and white pines. At 0.9 km (0.6 mile) you reach another overlook where the Buffalo Nut Trail comes in from the right. A picturesque white pine stands at the edge of the cliff. A bit farther, look for an old lightning scar on a white pine to the left of the trail. You can hear but not see Entrance Rapids from this point.

Oakwoods Trail comes in from the right at 1.1 km (0.7 mile), and shortly, at a large white pine, there is a side trail that leads to the edge of the river. Back on the Ferncliff Trail, ignore the next side trail, as it does not lead to any good view. At 1.9 km (1.2 miles) keep left; the Fernwood Trail diverges to the right. The trail returns to the cliff side and you can hear another rapids below. An unsigned trail goes right at 2.4 km (1.5 miles), and soon you turn left to an overlook that provides a good view of the rapids.

At 2.7 km (1.7 miles) bear right and the trail will take you through a stand of hemlock set about with boulders. From here you can hear the roar of yet another rapids—probably Railroad Rapids. Next, turn right to take the trail back across the base of Ferncliff Peninsula. Along the way you cross a small meadow; bear left at the trail junction to return to your car.

For an unusual hike, follow the Takeout Trail loop to the foot of Railroad Rapids. Many river runners portage and put in again just below the falls. From the takeout you can see the Western Maryland Railroad bridge across the Yough. Note how much higher this bridge is than the one scarcely 600 meters away at the village of Ohiopyle. That's how much the river has fallen in its trip around the Ferncliff Natural Area.

Charles F. Lewis Natural Area

Distance: 8.I km (5 miles)
Time: 3½ hours
Rise: 410 meters (1340 feet)
Highlights: Views; waterfalls
Maps: USGS 7½' Vintondale; Gallitzin State Forest
Natural Area map

The Charles F. Lewis Natural Area is a small portion of Gallitzin State Forest located on Laurel Ridge northeast of the Conemaugh Gorge. Dr. Charles Fletcher Lewis, for whom the area is named, was a newspaperman, conservationist and first president of the Western Pennsylvania Conservancy.

The natural area, although only 155 hectares (385 acres), is suitably wild and rugged. It is reported to have an abundance of rattlesnakes and I think one buzzed at me on my first hike. Reptiles and amphibians are protected within the Natural Area. I also encountered a pileated woodpecker. At one point in the trail I was confronted by a large black object. Then it moved and snorted and I realized it was a bear. At the sound of her snorts, her cubs (at least two) shot up a basswood tree, and I fumbled in my pack for a telephoto lens. Mama snorted again, the cubs quickly returned to the ground, and by the time I was ready they had all vanished into the woods. The trails are steep, rocky and wet, so hiking boots are in order.

The Charles F. Lewis Natural Area is located on PA 403 in the Conemaugh Gorge, 3.5 miles south of US 22 and 5.9 miles from the PA 56 junction in Johnstown. There is plenty of parking space.

To start the hike, head across the open picnic area and pass through the arch at the start of the yellow-blazed Clark Run Trail. At 140 meters bear right up the steps. You will return on the log bridge over Clark Run to your left. At 275 meters you can see the best of the waterfalls on the run. Trees growing in this part of the valley are basswood, beech and yellow birch. The steepest part of the climb is over by the time you reach a charcoal flat at 1.2 km (0.7 mile). There are many more of these charcoal flats on Laurel Ridge. They supplied charcoal to the iron industry in the nineteenth century. (Two charcoal iron furnaces can be seen in the New Florence game lands on Hike 15.)

A trail junction is reached at 1.3 km (0.8 mile). The yellow-blazed Clark Run Trail turns left on a woods road. Beware, the red-orange blazes of the Rager Mountain Trail are also present! To pick up the Rager Mountain Trail jog

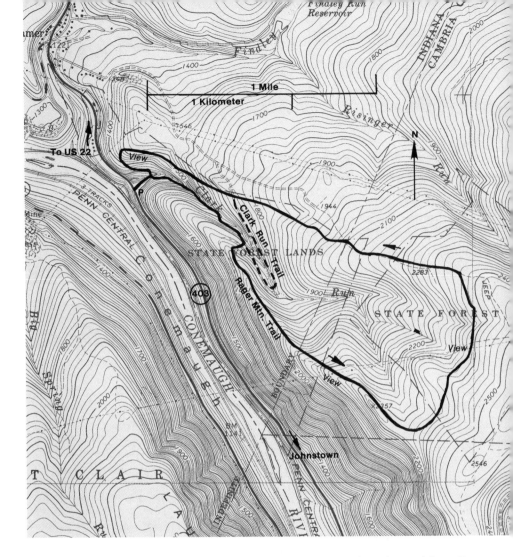

right 10 meters on the old road and
head up the flight of rotting steps. The
Rager Mountain Trail climbs the ridge
line between Clark Run and Conemaugh
Gorge. At 2.4 km (1.5 miles) cross a
power line swath that provides views of
Conemaugh Gorge and Laurel Ridge.

Continuing on the Rager Mountain
Trail the ridge becomes very narrow
and you pass an outcrop of cross-bed-
ded sandstone. The ridge then
broadens out as you approach the upper portions of Rager Mountain. At 3.3
km (2.1 miles) cross a snowmobile trail.

Just beyond there is a charcoal flat with
a pile of rotting logs. Was this flat to be
used in a demonstration of charcoal
making? Surely these logs can't have
survived from when this flat was actually
used.

Cross Rager Mountain Road at 3.6
km (2.2 miles) and recross a power line
swath at 4.1 km (2.5 miles). There is a
view down the Conemaugh River and
generally over the C.F. Lewis Natural
Area. Jog right on a snowmobile trail at
4.4 km (2.7 miles) and again at 4.8 km
(3.0 miles). The white-blazed state forest

Conemaugh Gorge

boundary is reached at 5.3 km (3.3 miles) and the trail parallels it for about 300 meters. Along this stretch a mysterious (not shown on any map) red-blazed trail takes off to the left.

At 6.5 km (4.0 miles) you reach the Clark Run Trail, which comes in from the left on an old road. To the right you can see a gate blocking the old road at the edge of state forest land. Follow the Clark Run Trail across the old road. This trail is rough and rocky as it cuts across the side of the valley and is an ideal place to meet rattlesnakes, so watch where you step. There are cliffs to the right and you pass through clumps of rhododendrons and mountain laurel. At 7.1 km (4.4 miles) you top out along the state forest boundary. A view rock to

the left is reached at 7.5 km (4.7 miles). It provides a view across Clark Run Valley and up Conemaugh Gorge.

Back on the trail, you soon turn left and descend steeply at times through very rocky terrain. At 7.8 km (4.8 miles) turn left on a road which is the old route of the paved highway. The original highway bridge over Clark Run is gone so you must bear left off the old highway and proceed upstream to the log bridge. Across the bridge bear right on the trail you came in on and you are soon back to your car.

Additional hiking opportunities in this area are Hike 8, on the other side of Conemaugh Gorge, and Hike 15, farther south near New Florence.

3

Wolf Rocks Trail

Distance: 7.3 km (4.5 miles)
Time: 2½ hours
Rise: 60 meters (200 feet)
Highlight: Panoramic view
Maps: USGS 7½' Ligonier, Bakersville; Forbes State Forest
  Public Use map

Natural overlooks are rare in Pennsylvania. Since no part of the state approaches timberline in elevation, rocky cliffs provide the only views. Such cliffs are uncommon, and trees below frequently grow tall enough to shut off the view. Laurel Hill is broad and flat on top, further reducing the chances for a natural overlook. This hike visits an overlook on Laurel Hill that surmounts all these obstacles and provides a 180-degree panorama above Linn Run.

The hike starts from Laurel Summit State Park, which is also the access point for the Spruce Flats Bog. The origin of this depression on top of Laurel Ridge is obscure. The bog had progressed to a mature stand of hemlock, which is frequently confused with spruce, when it was logged in 1908. It turned out that the transpiration of the trees had been responsible for removing the water from this undrained depression. With the trees gone, the water table rose and the bog was reformed. All efforts at reforestation have failed; to become forest again, the bog must repeat the natural succession.

The Laurel Summit State Park is 5.8 miles south of US 30 on the Laurel Summit road. Turn at the sign for Laurel Mountain Ski Resort. The park can also be reached from PA 381 at Rector via the Linn Run road. A picnic shelter and tables, as well as pit toilets, are available at the park.

The roads in the park appear to have been spurs on the Pittsburgh, Westmoreland and Somerset Railroad, which was built across Laurel Ridge at the turn of the century to serve the Byers-Allen sawmill at Ligonier. Chartering the railroad separately from the sawmill established it as a "common carrier" and permitted it to condemn rights of way when needed. Although the P, W & S eventually reached Somerset, using part of the right of way built for the South Penn railroad (Vanderbilt's Folly), its name can only have sprung from nineteenth century optimism, for it never had the remotest hope of reaching Pittsburgh. The South Penn right of way was owned at that time by the Baltimore and Ohio, which did not grant the P, W & S permission. Building the P, W & S without permission was an act of corporate chutzpah. The grades across Laurel Hill were stiff, but rod locomotives were able to negotiate them. Geared shay locomotives were used only on logging spurs where grades hit twelve percent.

The Wolf Rocks Trail is fairly flat and has rocks mostly at the far end. A loop has recently been added for cross country skiing. Ordinary walking shoes should be fine for this hike.

Head back through the picnic area and bear left to the corner where the blazes begin. The Wolf Rocks Trail is marked with both blue and red blazes. Parts of the trail have been relocated to make it better for skiing. At 0.3 km (0.2 mile) you cross a pipeline swath. The trail continues along the fringes of the Spruce Flats Bog, where rhododendron thrives. The bridge over a tiny stream has been replaced by a culvert but at 1.0 km (0.6 mile) you reach a signed trail junction. (The red-blazed Spruce Flats

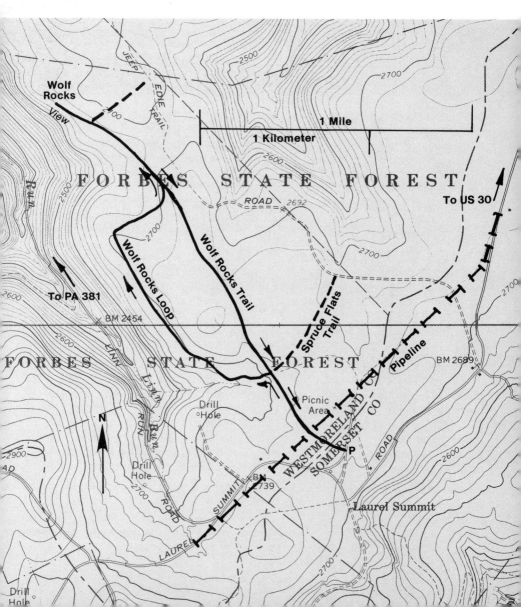

View from Wolf Rocks

Trail goes right here.) Turn left on the recently cut Wolf Rocks Loop, which is also red-blazed. Turn right at 2.5 km (1.5 miles) and then cross more culverts at 2.9 km (1.8 miles). Farther on, this ski trail has been bulldozed up a particularly rough section. At 3.4 km (2.1 miles) turn left on the old Wolf Rocks Trail at a signed junction. Next you cross an old road and arrive at Wolf Rocks at 3.9 km (2.4 miles). You can see down Linn Run Valley and across to Chestnut Ridge in the west. You can also see up Fish Run Valley, across from you, and to the top of Laurel Hill itself. Rhododendron and mountain ash trees grow around Wolf Rocks, adding to its appeal.

To return, follow the old Wolf Rocks Trail. Go straight ahead at 4.3 km (2.7 miles), pass a red-blazed trail to the left at 5.4 km (3.3 miles) which leads to Edie Road. Near 5.7 km (3.5 miles) trees have been cut to the left of the trail. At 6.3 km (3.9 miles), continue ahead at the other end of the Wolf Rocks Loop and retrace your steps to the picnic area.

There is a nearby hike at Linn Run State Park (Hike 4). The Laurel Highlands Hiking Trail runs to the east of the summit and can be reached by the P, W & S grade.

Linn Run State Park

Distance: 6.7 km (4.2 miles)
Time: 2¾ hours
Rise: 260 meters (850 feet)
Highlights: Waterfalls
Maps: USGS 7½' Ligonier; state park map

Linn Run State Park is a small state park on the western side of Laurel Hill. To the south is Forbes State Forest. These lands had been clearcut by the time the state purchased them from Byers and Allen Lumber Company in 1909. The Pittsburgh, Westmoreland and Somerset Railroad, built for the logging, had started many fires on the cutover land and the deer had all been killed. As a result, there was criticism of the state for spending money on such wasteland. Today, we are the beneficiaries of the state's foresight. Deer were reintroduced from Michigan and New York. The forest reclaimed the briar patches and fern fields. The Linn Run Road has almost obliterated the Pittsburgh, Westmoreland and Somerset Railroad. In the 1930s the Civilian Conservation Corps built many of the structures in the park. More recently, these have been rebuilt by the Youth Conservation Corps and Pennsylvania Conservation Corps.

The Youth Conservation Corps also built an attractive hiking trail up Grove Run, over the height of land to the east and down Boot Hollow Run. The trailhead is located at Grove Run Picnic Area, which is on the Linn Run Road

three miles southeast of the small village of Rector (on PA 38I). Ordinary walking shoes should be fine for this short hike.

Drive through the picnic area, which is equipped with a piped spring and restrooms, and park in the small area at the far end. The blue-blazed Grove Run Trail begins here. Pass around the vehicle gate and step across the outlet from a spring to the right of the trail. The Grove Run Trail was built as a nature trail complete with numbered posts. Today most of the posts are missing. The trail starts out easily along an old logging road, but at 0.6 km (0.4 mile) you bear right and climb up the side of the valley. Trees along this section of the trail are tulip, red oak and red maple.

Farther along, the stream, which often flows underground in the lower parts of the valley, returns to the surface. After you cross Grove Run on a bridge just below a small pool, swing left and climb up the valley of a tributary. Next, you pass a waterfall that can be seen and heard in the narrow valley below. Trees along this stretch are basswood, sugar maple, beech and striped maple (*acer*

Pool on Grove Run

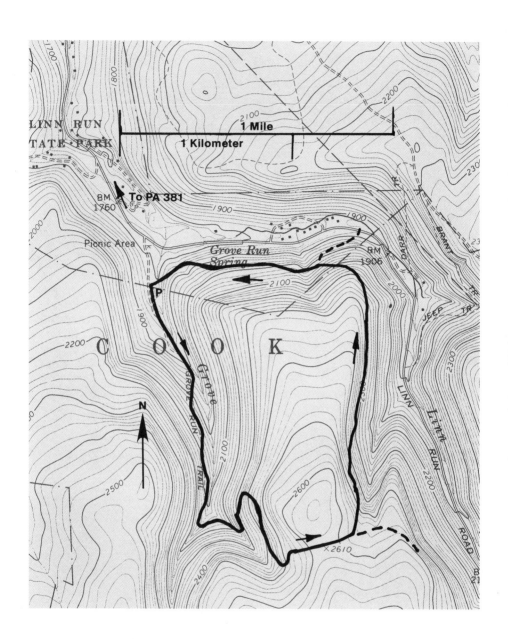

pennsylvanicum). Soon you cross the
spot where most of the tributary comes
down across mossy ledges to the right
of the trail; then at 2.0 km (1.3 miles)
turn left across the remainder of the
stream and continue climbing across the
hillside. The trail switchbacks up the
steep slope. The abundance of greenbrier, a vine-like thorny plant, discour-
ages you from shortcutting the switchbacks. Despite its thorns, greenbrier, or
catbrier, is food for deer, bear, grouse,

turkey and smaller animals. On these drier slopes chestnut oak is the most common tree.

There is a trail register at the end of one switchback. If the register had been placed closer to the road, almost certainly it would have gone the way of the numbered trail posts. Take the time to register. You still have some climbing ahead, so this is a good place for a breather.

After another switchback, you cross a new logging road and reach the top of the hill at 2.9 km (1.8 miles) and cross the Quarry Trail. Just beyond keep left where another blue-blazed trail diverges to the right and ultimately leads to Fish Run. A sign is to be installed at this junction. Soon you cross a watercourse and start down into Boot Hollow. The trail cuts along the side of the steep slope, where there should be some leaves-off views across Linn Run Valley. In summer the green curtain is opaque. At 4.7 km (2.9 miles) cross the corner of an old blowdown. Wild grapevines have taken over and

produced a tangle that is now encroaching on the surrounding trees. The wild grapes provide food and cover for wildlife, particularly birds.

Cross the snowmobile trail again and at 5.4 km (3.3 miles) bear left on a new trail cut by volunteers in 1989. This trail, which is also blue-blazed, avoids walking on the Linn Run Road by traversing the hillside above Linn Run. If you reach a switchback you have missed this turn. The new trail soon passes above a spring and picks up an old footway but mostly it is all new. It descends slowly and then crosses Grove Run. A foot bridge will be built here if a permit can be obtained. The trail continues to the piped spring in Grove Run Picnic Area.

Two short hikes are found farther up Linn Run. On the north side, the Darr Trail and Brant Trail make a short loop, using part of the old Rector Edie Road. On the south side, the Fish Run Trail leads to the remains of the Pittsburgh, Westmoreland and Somerset Railroad. You can also make a loop by returning along Fish Run.

Mt. Davis Natural Area

Distance: 9.4 km (5.8 miles)
Time: 3½ hours
Rise: 225 meters (740 feet)
Highlight: Highest point in Pennsylvania; mountain laurel and
*   rhododendron*
Maps: USGS 7½' Markleton; public use map—Forbes State
*   Forest*

Of the states in the Appalachian Mountains, Pennsylvania has the lowest high point. At 979 meters (3,230 feet), it is a serious disappointment to peak baggers. Yet Mt. Davis has character. Unlike the highest point of one midwestern state, it is not in the middle of a cornfield. The trees are stunted; even on a sunny day it has an alpine feel, but the weather is frequently foul—even in midsummer there can be fog so thick that you can't see the ground from the top of the 15 meter observation tower.

Mt. Davis Natural Area is 235 hectares (580.5 acres) of state forest surrounding the high point on Negro Mountain. The peak is named for an early settler and former owner of the area, while legend has it that the mountain is named for a black man who was killed there when he and his companions were set upon by Indians or by a wounded bear or other wild animal. The incident may have taken place to the south, in Maryland, where Negro Mountain reaches a higher elevation.

This is a circuit hike using the Mt. Davis picnic area on LR (Legislative Route) 55008 as a trailhead. The picnic area is 9.2 miles from Meyersdale,

which in turn is about 22 miles south of Somerset on US 219. In Meyersdale, turn west on Broadway Street and follow the occasional signs for Mt. Davis. A bit west of town you can see Negro Mountain ahead of you, particularly the large microwave relay tower that is just across the road from the picnic area. Coming from the west on US 40, turn north on PA 523 for 1.5 miles, then turn east in Listonburg. Pass High Point and Deer Valley lakes to reach the picnic area and trailhead at 10.7 miles from Listonburg. The high point of Mt. Davis itself could be used as an alternative trailhead, which would shorten the hike by 0.6 km (0.4 mile). Outhouses and a pump for drinking water are available at the picnic area. The picnic area and much of the land covered on the Tub Mill Run Trail were added to Forbes State Forest after the USGS map was printed.

To start your hike, head uphill to the top of the picnic area and then turn left on the High Point Trail. At 0.3 km (0.2 mile) turn left on the blue-blazed Tub Mill Run Trail. This junction was unsigned and the blazes faded on my last visit but they are still fairly easy to find.

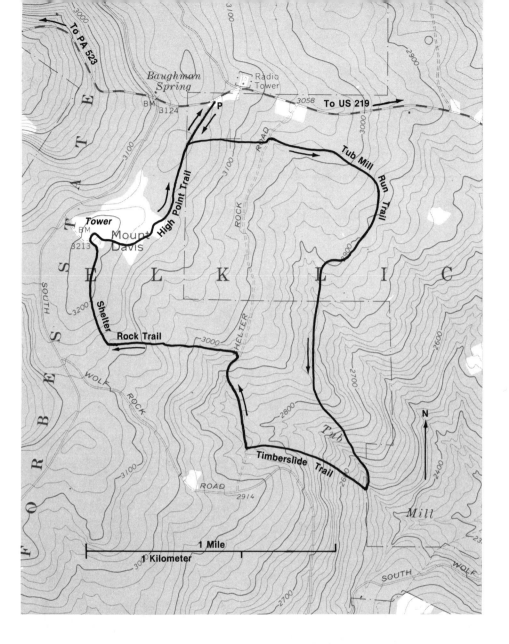

Jog left across Shelter Rock Road at 0.9 km (0.6 mile) to continue on the same trail. You descend gently through banks of rhododendron and mountain laurel. The trail emerges at the edge of a pipeline swath that follows the eastern boundary of state forest land. At 2.7 km (1.7 miles) you reach the edge of a small cliff set about with mountain laurel and rhododendron. Soon you cross a nameless tributary of Tub Mill Run and continue through the forest to 4.1 km (2.6 miles) where the trail parallels Tub Mill Run itself, which jumps from rock to rock under the rhododendron. When the water is even moderately high this is a

A GEOLOGIC FEATURE

MT. DAVIS

MT. DAVIS 3213 FEET ABOVE SEA LEVEL
IS THE HIGHEST POINT IN PENNSYLVANIA.
THE EROSION-RESISTANT SANDSTONE AT THE
SURFACE BELONGS TO THE POTTSVILLE GROUP
FORMED ABOUT 230 MILLION YEARS AGO.
THESE LAYERS OF SEDIMENTARY ROCK WERE
PUSHED UP AS AN UPFOLD 200 MILLION YEARS
AGO DURING THE UPHEAVAL CALLED THE
APPALACHIAN REVOLUTION.

delightful stream. At 4.6 km (2.9 miles) you cross Tub Mill Run. Even with moderately low water the stepping stones are covered so the crossing can be exciting.

The trail continues briefly down the far side of the run before climbing to a junction with the Timberslide Trail at the edge of a clearcut dating from the mid 1980s. Turn right and start the climb up to Mt. Davis. There are occasional blue blazes along the Timberslide Trail. At the top edge of the clearcut there is a view to the east and south. At 5.5 km (3.4 miles) you turn right on the Shelter Rock Road, which is closed to vehicles. Soon you pass Wildcat Spring, a few paces to the right of the road—the water comes up through the sand so fast that it looks as if it was boiling. Cross a bridge over Tub Mill Run—not nearly so exciting as your last crossing—and at 6.1 km (3.8 miles) you turn left on the Shelter Rock Trail. This trail is very straight, and a good deal of work has been done on the footway. Cross Tub Mill Run for the last time and then pass Shelter Rock to your left. At 6.6 km (4.1 miles) you reach the top of the hill. The trail takes you through a forest of stunted trees: black gum, pitch pine, oak, aspen, sassafras and maple. It's not just the poor soil on the Pottsville

sandstone, but the many ice storms and the generally inclement weather that keep these trees so small.

At 7.7 km (4.8 miles) the Mt. Davis Trail diverges to the right, providing a very short loop on top of Mt. Davis. Turn left and then right on the paved road to reach the base of the observation tower. If weather permits, climb the tower for commanding views in all directions. The view from the tower includes stone circles to the north. These are formed when frost heaves elevate an area of soft soil and, over the years, the rocks gradually slide down the sides. The ridge is so flat that points to the north and south actually appear higher than Mt. Davis. Careful surveying shows them to be lower, but it is a convincing optical illusion.

Continue to the exhibits and cross the paved road to pick up the High Point Trail. The Mt. Davis Trail soon comes from your right and next you are back under larger trees. At 9.0 km (5.6 miles) you pass the junction with the Tub Mill Run Trail, and it is a short distance to the parking lot.

Additional hiking opportunities are found south of the Natural Area on the Livengood, Wolf Rock, and Laurel Run trails, totalling over six kilometers (3.7 miles).

Mt. Davis Lookout Tower

Cucumber and Jonathan Run Falls

Distance: 9.5 km (5.9 miles)
Time: 3½ hours
Rise: 135 meters (440 feet)
Highlights: Waterfalls; spring wildflowers
Maps: USGS 7½' South Connellsville, Mill Run, Fort Necessity,
  Ohiopyle; state park map

A tram road is a railroad that uses geared locomotives. Geared locomotives were developed for the nineteenth century logging industry. Coal mining also involved heavy loads and steep grades, problems frequently solved with a tram railroad even into the first decades of the twentieth century. This hike uses the grade of one such old railroad, now part of the Great Gorge Trail along Cucumber Run and the Youghiogheny River.

This hike requires a short car shuttle. Drive west on L.R. (Legislative Route) 26071 for 1.4 miles from the log cabin on PA 381 in Ohiopyle State Park. Continue ahead at the junction at the top of the hill for 1.6 miles more to a small parking lot on Jonathan Run and leave one car here. Then drive back 2.6 miles to the Cucumber Falls parking area. (In times of high water leave a car either at the Old Mitchell Place or at a lot across from the campground near the end of T-796. See park map.)

There is a bridgeless crossing of Cucumber Run near the start of this hike. This can be avoided by crossing the one-lane bridge above Cucumber Falls and turning right on the Great Gorge Trail at the far side. Numerous wet spots and rocks make hiking boots better for this hike. However, with a little care, good walking shoes should do.

To start, descend the steps on the north side of the road. At the first level you get the best view of the falls of the Cucumber. Continue down the switchbacks to the Yough and a junction with Meadow Run Trail. Turn left and hunt for a spot where Cucumber Run is funneled between two large rocks. Here you can jump across. Keep left, pick up the yellow blazes, and follow the Meadow Run Trail as it climbs away from the Yough and ends at the Great Gorge Trail.

Turn right on this old tram road and follow it past one of the old coal mines. At 1.6 km (1.0 mile) you have to get off the railroad grade to cross a ravine. The bridge is long gone. The best displays of spring wildflowers are found along the Great Gorge Trail. Somewhere beyond here the railroad ended, but a road continued to more mines farther along the gorge. At 2.2 km (1.4 miles) you reach a junction with the Beech

Cucumber Falls

Trail, and the Great Gorge Trail climbs the hill to the campground. Another trail connects with the Western Maryland Railroad grade. Continue on the Beech Trail. On the white-blazed Beech Trail at 2.6 km (1.6 miles) you come to another old coal mine, and at 3.4 km (2.1 miles) to a rock overhang, a good place to wait out a shower.

At 4.2 km (2.6 miles) where the Beech Trail turns uphill, turn right and descend steeply to the Western Maryland Railroad grade. Turn left on the grade and look out for bicycles. With the completion of the bicycle trail upstream from Ohiopyle, bicycle usage at Ohiopyle State Park rose to equal the whitewater usage. With the completion of this downstream bicycle trail, whitewater usage will drop to second place. Despite all the trails in the park, hiking will be a distant third.

At 4.9 km (3.0 miles) you pass a small post that bears the letters NN which stand for No Name rapids. If a river runner is injured, help would be summoned by radio. The emergency vehicles would follow the Western Maryland Railroad grade to the rapids where the accident occurred. Since you usually can't see the river from the railroad grade, these posts tell the drivers where to stop.

Next the grade passes cliffs on the inside of a bend. Dimples and Swimmers rapids (DS) is passed at 6.0 km (3.7 miles) and Bottle of Wine (BW) at 6.5 km (4.0 miles).

At 7.0 km (4.3 miles) turn left on the Kentuck Trail. There is no sign, but the trail is marked with blue blazes and a small pile of gravel. If you miss this turn, the Western Maryland grade crosses a high fill above Jonathan Run. Back on the Kentuck Trail, bear right at 7.2 km (4.5 miles) for the best view of Jonathan Run Falls.

Continue ahead on the blue-blazed Jonathan Run Trail at 7.6 km (4.7 miles) where the Kentuck Trail turns uphill. Cross Jonathan Run or the footbridges at 7.7 km (4.8 miles) and again at 8.1 km (5.0 miles).

Continuing up Jonathan Run you pass a clearing at 8.4 km (5.2 miles) with an old apple tree. Just beyond, climb the bank and follow a relocation to avoid further crossings of Jonathan Run. At 8.9 km (5.5 miles) turn sharply left and follow another relocation to avoid a water damaged section of the old grade. After rejoining the old grade continue upstream to the parking lot for Jonathan Run Trail.

This hike could be extended by returning to the Western Maryland grade after viewing Jonathan Run Falls. Follow the grade across Jonathan Run and continue for a few hundred meters to Sugar Run. Turn left on a new trail cut by Keystone Trails Association Trail Care team in July 1989 for an intimate view of Sugar Run Falls. Continue up the new trail and turn left at the top to reach the river runners parking lot at the old Mitchell Place. Leave a car at this parking lot if you intend to take this option. The Sugar Run or Kentuck options would involve more climbing than the one described here. Other hikes at Ohiopyle State Park are described in Hikes 1, 13 and 14.

7

Little Run Trail

Distance: 13 km (8 miles)
Time: 4¾ hours
Rise: 345 meters (1,130 feet)
Highlights: Mountain stream
Maps: USGS 7½' Seven Springs, Bakersville

Between the Pennsylvania Turnpike and PA 31 lies another part of Forbes State Forest that used to be part of the Western Pennsylvania Conservancy's Mountain Streams tract as is Roaring Run. This is the valley of Little Run. There are no blazes, trail signs or even road signs in or around Little Run so it should not be attempted until you have some experience at pathfinding. Repeated stream crossings and wet spots call for hiking boots on this hike and it should be made only at low water.

To reach the trailhead, turn north on the Quarry Road from PA 31. The junction is on the east slope of Laurel Hill, just 0.3 mile west of Hidden Valley Ski Area and directly across from an active stone quarry. Drive north on the Quarry Road, crossing the Laurel Highlands Hiking Trail, for 1.5 miles to a junction with a nameless forestry Road. Park along the side of the road.

To start the hike, go down the Quarry Road ahead. Note the appearance of permanent puddles and ledges in the road as its quality deteriorates. Soon you pass a small springhouse on the left. At 0.7 km (0.4 mile) avoid an obvious old road to the left that is blocked by a wooden gate. Hold out for the real

Little Run Trail that diverges left about 100 meters farther on. This trail is blocked with boulders to encourage compliance with the ATV law. With their persistent disregard of all regulations and relentless production of mud holes, All Terrain Vehicles (ATV's) have developed an image problem. There are also a number of artificial blowdowns. Soon you cross a pair of natural gas pipelines. There is another boulder barrier beyond the second pipeline, but ATV's have made their way around it. Such passive defenses seem entirely futile.

At 1.7 km (1.1 miles) the trail passes through an old meadow that now is filled with goldenrod and hawthorn. This old road does not have a sufficiently constant grade to be a railroad, but it may have been a charcoal road. What may have been a charcoal flat is passed at 2.5 km (1.6 miles). At 3.2 km (2.0 miles) ignore an old road to the left, but bear left at 3.3 km (2.1 miles) where a woods road comes in from the right.

The Pennsylvania Turnpike is in the next valley to the north and you can hear its muted roar along this part of the Little Run Trail. Bear left again at 4.3 km (2.7 miles) where another trail comes in

from the right and ignore another trail from the right at 4.6 km (2.9 miles). By now the Little Run Trail is on the crest of the ridge and individual trucks can be heard on the turnpike. The old road becomes increasingly eroded with ledges of bedrock exposed but a strategically placed barrier has still failed to stop the ATV incursions.

At 5.8 km (3.6 miles) cross an old logging railroad and continue downhill past more barriers, that have stopped pickup trucks, to turn left on another railroad grade along Indian Creek. Note the cinders in the railroad bed. At 6.3 km (3.9 miles) cross Little Run as best you can and turn left on a rough trail at 6.7 km (4.2 miles). Avoid a trail to the right just 100 meters farther on. After climbing a bit the trail follows along the side of Little Run. Little Run tumbles over moss-covered rocks as it flows among the rhododendrons. From its straightness and even grade you can deduce that it has picked up an old railroad grade, probably the one you crossed back at 5.8 km (3.6 miles).

At 7.7 km (4.8 miles) there is a pair of crossings of Little Run. At 8.1 km (5 miles) avoid a trail to the right. Cross a side stream and then Little Run two more times. At 8.6 km (5.3 miles) pass a trail to the left and then keep right to avoid crossing Little Run. Ignore a trail to the right and cross Little Run at 8.9 km (5.5 miles). Then ignore two more trails to the right and one to the left and cross Little Run again.

At 9.3 km (5.8 miles) leave the old railroad grade and turn right into a gas well clearing. Continue across the clearing and follow the access road up the valley.

At 10.1 km (6.3 miles) cross Little Run

Boulders blocking jeep road

again and in another 100 meters turn right on a gas line road. Ahead the pipeline you have been following climbs steeply. Cross Little Run for the last time on a culvert, pass a steel gate and then bear right on a larger gas line road. This road climbs out of Little Run valley by way of a hollow to the south. Near the top this road bears left in an old clearing which has been invaded by hawthorn. After passing another boulder barrier, turn left on a nameless but little used forestry road at 11.3 km (7.0 miles).

At 12.2 km (7.6 miles) there is a road right into a large clearcut, followed by a good climb to the top of the ridge where the road turns right along the top of the clearcut. There are occasional views west over the valley to Chestnut Ridge.

Turn left at 12.7 km (7.9 miles) to avoid a private road ahead, cross a gas pipe line and follow this nameless forestry road back to your car just over the summit.

Additional hiking opportunities can be found at Roaring Run south of PA 31 (Hike 9), Laurel Hill State Park (Hike 10) and the Kincora Trail at Kooser State Park, just down the hill on PA 31.

Conemaugh Gorge

In-and-out distance: 11.5 km (7.2 miles)
Time: 4 hours
Rise: 365 meters (1200 feet)
Highlight: Views
Maps: USGS 7½′ New Florence, Vintondale; Laurel Ridge
  State Park map; "Hikers Guide to the Laurel Highlands
  Trail," map 12

One of the most prominent geographic features in western Pennsylvania is Laurel Hill. Stretching north from the Mason-Dixon Line and reaching elevations up to 900 meters, Laurel Hill forms a barrier to transportation across the state. Even its modest elevation is enough to measurably alter the climate on the hill. The annual temperature averages about three degrees Celsius lower, and total precipitation about 50% higher, than flanking areas. Snowfall can be five times as great.

Nature provided only two gaps through Laurel Hill, the Youghiogheny in the south and the Conemaugh in the north. Presumably these gaps were eroded by water as the land was slowly uplifted. The streams may appear inadequate for the task, but a stream does almost all its eroding when it is at flood stage.

Conemaugh Gorge must have presented an appalling sight during the Johnstown Flood of 1889. On the afternoon of 31 May the South Fork Dam burst. The ruins just east of US 219 are preserved as a national historic site. The flood swept through Johnstown killing over 2,200 people. Much of the debris piled up on the old stone bridge in Johnstown where many burned to death, but there must have been more that was carried through Conemaugh Gorge. Bodies were found as far downstream as Pittsburgh.

In the nineteenth century both the Pennsylvania Canal and the Pennsylvania Railroad used the Conemaugh Gorge to get through Laurel Ridge. Later railroad development appears to have obliterated the canal in the gorge. The highways go right over the top. Even the turnpike climbs over the ridge in preference to using the old South Penn Railroad tunnel. As there is no practical car shuttle, this is an in-and-out hike. The views are best when the leaves are off.

The trailhead for this hike is reached from PA 56. The turnoff (on the south side of PA 56) is 1.0 mile east of the junction of PA 711 in Seward and about 4.8 miles from Johnstown. The parking area is 0.4 mile from PA 56 and drink-

Conemaugh Gorge

ing water is available from a fountain in summer. A sign warns that cars are left at the owner's risk. The footway is good to excellent so walking shoes should be adequate for this hike.

Moving into the woods on the yellow-blazed Laurel Highlands Trail, you quickly come to a concrete marker embedded in the ground and labeled number 70. This is the last milepost on the Laurel Highlands Trail. Actually the Laurel Highlands Trail isn't quite 70 miles long, so the last mile was shortened by about one-third to accommodate milepost 70.

Next, you encounter a trail register. Even day hikers should register as funding for maintenance depends on usage. Overnight use of the shelter areas requires a reservation, which can be made by calling (412) 455-3744. Shortly, the trail crosses a jeep road to

the Big Spring Reservoir which can be seen to the right. A great many communities get their drinking water from the flanks of Laurel Ridge.

At 1.0 km (0.6 mile) there is a wooden-poled power line. To the left, you can catch a glimpse of Conemaugh Gorge. But the best views are to come. After crossing a jeep road in back of a spoil bank, you come to milepost 69. The jeep road crosses once again as the trail approaches the edge of the gorge. Note the rhododendrons growing on the moist north-facing slope of the gorge. Soon you reach the first real view. Across the gorge you see the Charles F. Lewis Natural Area and the valley of Clark Run. Towering above is Rager Mountain. Note the mountain laurel, for which the ridge is named. There is evidence of quarrying along this section. At one point, a large steel bolt pro-

trudes from a sandstone boulder. At another point, there are cinders in the trail, presumably from a steam engine at the top of a funicular used to lower stone to the bottom of the gorge. Small trees here are sassafras and large ones are tulip.

At 2.3 km (1.5 miles) you cross the corner of a jeep road, leaving the quarry area and its views. Soon you come to a 500 kilovolt power line on steel pylons. To the left, there is a spectacular view of the gorge, while on the right you can see the coal-fired power plant producing the power. You come next to milepost 68, and just beyond that there is a large red oak growing on the brink of the gorge. At about 4.0 km (2.5 miles) the trail levels off but still follows the edge of the abyss. Milepost 67 is passed at 4.4 km (2.8 miles). Small trees growing along here are striped maple; many of the large ones are black cherry, the premier northern hardwood. It has a dark, flaky bark. The ground underneath may be covered with the pits of the cherries of past years.

At about 5 km (3 miles) the trail starts to climb again with leaves-off views of the east end of the gorge, where you can see parts of Johnstown; Rager Mountain can also be seen beyond the gorge.

The trail soon swings away from the edge of the gorge and heads south near the crest of Laurel Hill. A jeep road is reached at 5.8 km (3.6 miles), which marks the end of the views. Lower Yoder firetower is 0.6 mile farther. Because of repeated vandalism it has been fenced off so its views of Johnstown and Laurel Ridge are no longer available. Retrace your steps to your car. Hiking a trail in the other direction frequently doubles what you see.

Roaring Run Natural Area

Distance: 13.2 km (8.2 miles)
Time: 5 hrs
Rise: 375 meters (1230 feet)
Highlights: Mountain stream; spring wildflowers
Maps: USGS 7½' Seven Springs; State Forest Natural Area
*   map*

At 1,450 hectares (3,582 acres) Roaring Run is the largest state forest natural area in western Pennsylvania. It is part of the mountain streams tract that was purchased by the Western Pennsylvania Conservancy on the western slopes of Laurel Ridge and transferred to Forbes State Forest in 1975. Before the Conservancy acquired the tract, a good deal of logging had been carried out. It will take a century for the second- and third-growth hardwood forest to mature, but hikers of the late twenty-first century have a real treat in store.

The trailhead can be reached entirely on paved roads. Owing to frequent crossings of Roaring Run, this hike should be attempted only during low water. Hiking boots and long pants which protect your legs from briars are a must. The best time to visit Roaring Run for spring wildflowers is the last two weeks in April.

To reach the trailhead from PA 31, turn south on PA 381 and PA 711 at Jones Mills. After 1.1 miles turn east (left) on County Line Road at the gas station in Champion. Then go 1.8 miles to a small parking area on the left side of the road.

To start your hike, walk around the vehicle gate and head up the old woods road. Much of this hike is on similar old roads, and although the natural area is closed to motor vehicles, the ruts you will see in every wet spot show frequent ATV incursions. The trail is marked with faded blue blazes.

At 0.5 km (0.3 mile) you continue ahead where the South Loop Trail comes in from the right. Further on, the old road crosses a culvert over a small stream. Catbriers flourish in the undergrowth here. They can make off-trail hiking very painful, but are a favorite food of the deer. Where the trail cuts across a steep slope, note the boulders that have slid down the mountain.

At 1.5 km (0.9 mile) you pass an intersection with the Painter Rock Trail and then cross Roaring Run. This is the first of 28 stream crossings, and if this one does not appear feasible, you had best retreat and just hike up and back on the South Loop Trail. Turn right and continue up Roaring Run.

After the second stream crossing, look for rhododendrons growing along the run. They should bloom in early July or a glorious fall day.

The straightness of the trail along Roaring Run shows it was a logging railroad. Near 2.3 km (1.4 miles) look for a basswood tree growing along the run. Basswood can be recognized by its nearly circular or heartshaped leaves and its seeds which are borne in a cluster attached to a narrow leaflike blade or sail. Although basswood is classed as a hardwood its wood is actually soft and suitable for carving. The Iroquois carved masks from a living tree, and when the outside was finished split the masks off to hollow out the back. Using live wood must have increased the medicine or spiritual power of the mask.

A small meadow is reached at 2.8 km (1.7 miles) and you next cross two small streams from the south. After this, the crossings of Roaring Run become more frequent. At about 4 km (2.5 miles) the trail really starts to climb and the stream is much reduced in size. There is a double crossing at 4.8 km (3.0 miles). These two crossings are some of the very few on this hike that could be avoided without excessive bushwhacking. The next eight crossings come in quick order as the valley is constricted by steep banks.

At 5.4 km (3.4 miles) double blazes announce the junction with the Painter Rock Trail. There is also a sign nailed to a tree and a campsite near the stream. If you miss the Painter Rock Trail you will next meet the even more obscure junction with the South Loop and then reach a parking lot on the Fire Tower Road. Turn left on the Painter Rock Trail, which is also blue-blazed, and cross Roaring Run once again. Turn sharp left and climb the stream bank on a rough footway. At the top of the hill the footway improves and soon you pick up an old woods road that leads to a clearing.

Just beyond the clearing a red-blazed cross-country ski trail comes in from the

right on a jeep road. The Painter Rock Trail continues ahead on this jeep road. At 6.6 km (4.1 miles) there is a marker to the right of the trail for D.A. Sheets, C.K. Baker and Catherine Saylor who were killed on 19 January 1896 in a sleigh accident on their way home from church.

The blue- and red-blazed trail bears to the right on an old woods road. At 7.1 km (4.4 miles) keep right at an obscure junction where a previous route of the Painter Rock Trail goes left, but was never deblazed. Continue to the top of the ridge to an unsigned junction with the McKenna Trail. Turn left here and follow the red and blue blazes around the high point of Painter Rock Hill on an old woods road.

At 8.5 km (5.3 miles) turn right and follow the blue blazes uphill. The red-blazed cross-country ski trail continues downhill on the old woods road. Cross a tiny stream and pass a walled spring before reaching a woods road. Turn right and follow it uphill to a junction with the North Loop Trail at 8.8 km (5.5 miles).

Turn left at this unsigned junction and continue on the Painter Rock Trail along an old woods road. At 9.5 km (5.9 miles) turn left at the entrance to a clearing and continue on a less well-defined woods road. Then turn left again onto rocky trail at 9.7 km (6.0 miles). Next you pass a small cliff to the left; catbrier begins to encroach on the trail. At 10.5 km (6.5 miles) you reach a view over Roaring Run from the brink of a cliff, but the trail is largely overgrown with catbrier. This is where your long pants earn their keep.

Before you reach a junction with the North Loop at 10.8 km (6.7 miles) the catbrier has generally receded from the trail.

Continue downhill along the edge of

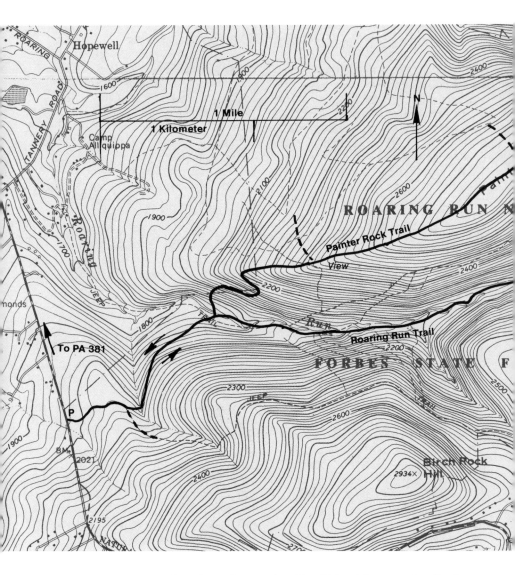

Painter Rock and then follow the trail down a series of rough switchbacks to a last crossing of Roaring Run at 11.6 km (7.2 miles). A few meters beyond the run turn right on the Roaring Run Trail and retrace your steps for 1.5 km (0.9 mile) to your car.

Other hiking opportunities in the Roaring Run Natural Area are the South Loop, which forms a circuit across the slopes of Birch Rock Hill, and the McKenna Trail, which leads out to Fire Tower Road near PA 31. Also the Laurel Highlands Trail crosses the southeastern corner of the natural area.

10

Laurel Hill State Park

Distance: 12.4 km (7.7 miles)
Time: 4½ hours
Rise: 230 meters (760 feet)
Highlights: Old-growth hemlock; Laurel Hill Lake
Maps: USGS 7½' Bakersville, Seven Springs, Rockwood; state park map

Laurel Hill State Park, in Somerset County, ranks as one of the larger parks in western Pennsylvania, having almost 1,600 hectares (4,000 acres). In the 1930s, Laurel Hill was one of five federal demonstration parks in Pennsylvania. The others were Raccoon, Blue Knob, Hickory Run and French Creek. After World War II these parks were transferred to the Commonwealth, with the stipulation that they continue to be used for recreation. Two of the nine group camps at Laurel Hill were once Civilian Conservation Corps camps. Do not confuse Laurel Hill State Park, which is in Laurel Hill Creek valley, with Laurel Ridge State Park, which is on top of the hill, or with Laurel Mountain State Park, which is a downhill ski area north of the Turnpike.

Laurel Hill State Park can be reached from PA 31, just east of Bakersville, by traveling south on LR (Legislative Route) 55052 for 1.7 miles to the eastern park entrance. The park can also be reached from PA 281 at New Centerville by driving west on LR 55049 for about 4 miles to the southern park entrance, just beyond an Exxon station and a Red and White food store. This hike starts from the large beach parking area, which is on the main park road connecting these two entrances, 0.7 mile from the south entrance and 2.8 miles from the east entrance. Stream crossings, rocks and wet spots suggest boots for this hike.

Begin the hike by heading north along the park road. At the first road junction bear left on the road to group camp 8, which appears to be an old CCC camp, and go around the vehicle gate. To the left of where this road enters the woods there are some graves which predate the park. At the far end of the group camp, continue straight ahead into the woods on a snowmobile trail, avoiding the road to the left. The ridge trail comes up from the right at 0.8 km (0.5 mile), and soon the aqueduct diverges to the right. Trail junctions in this park are frequently not signed. Soon a trail comes in from the left, and at 1.2 km (0.8 mile) you turn right on the Pump House Trail and descend gently to Jones Mill Run. At 1.7 km (1.1 miles) you cross the run on a snowmobile bridge and immediately turn left on the Tram Road Trail. This was the route of a logging railroad, operated by the United Lumber Company, that hauled logs to a sawmill at Humbert, near the confluence of Laurel Hill Creek and the Casselman River. The Tram Road Trail is marked with orange blazes of variable size and shape.

Next you come to a crossing of Jones Mill Run. If the water is high, you can avoid this crossing by bearing right because the Tram Road Trail soon returns to this side. Farther upstream there is another crossing that can also be avoided since the Tram Road Trail recrosses the run opposite the ruins of the old pump house and just below the small dam.

The pond behind the dam is a popular spot with fishermen. Avoid the trail fishermen have worn along the edge of the pond. Instead keep left on the Tram Road Trail where the Pump House Trail joins it from the right. At 3.7 km (2.3 miles) cross the aqueduct and immediately turn left on the Martz Trail.

At 4.0 km (2.5 miles) the Martz Trail meets the Beltz Road, which forms the border between Laurel Hill State Park and Forbes State Forest. This junction is signed but the Beltz Road is not. Turn right on the Beltz Road, ignoring a logging road which soon diverges to the

Jones Mill Run Dam

left. At 4.4 km (2.8 miles) turn right on the Bobcat Trail. This junction is obscure, but is marked with a trail sign on the left side of the road. If you miss this turn, you will cross a stream and come to the corner of a selective cut farther along the Beltz Trail, followed by a snowmobile trail to the left and a sign for Kooser State Park. Finding the Bobcat Trail will test your pathfinding skill.

The Bobcat Trail is getting harder to follow as its footway is blocked with frequent blowdowns and the occasional blazes of red or yellow are fading away. Maintenance has been deferred on the Bobcat. At 5.0 km (3.1 miles) you cross Buck Run. Shortly beyond the crossing, there is a spring to the right of the trail. Farther on, the trail parallels Buck Run, eventually crossing several tributaries. At 6.3 km (3.9 miles) turn left on Buck Run Road and you will soon pass the Boy Scout Buck Run High Adventure Camp. Turn right at 6.6 km (4.1 miles) on the yellow-blazed Hemlock Trail, cross Buck Run and turn left at a fork in the trail.

Four acres of virgin hemlock are found at 6.9 km (4.3 miles). As usual with small patches of old-growth trees in Penns Woods, the manner of their survival is not known. If a logger cut his neighbor's timber, he had to pay triple damages. So unless he had complete confidence in his surveyor, he was better off leaving uncut any small tracts of doubtful ownership. Perhaps these four acres are another monument to poor surveying. Ignore three blue-blazed trails (not shown on the park map) to the right along this section.

The trail continues along a secluded section of Laurel Hill Creek. At 7.9 km (4.9 miles) turn left on the paved park road, cross the bridge over Laurel Hill Creek, and then turn right on the Lake Trail. This is your last chance to shorten this hike by walking back along the park road. An old trailside shelter soon appears on the slope above the lake. This shelter was built of chestnut logs by the Civilian Conservation Corps before World War II. The roof is in bad shape and it no longer provides any effective shelter. Farther along is a piped spring, where camping is not permitted.

The Lake Trail continues along the steep east side of Laurel Hill Lake. Sometimes it follows almost at the water's edge but often climbs far up the slope. At 9.9 km (6.2 miles) you reach the spillway, but there is no bridge across the creek here. The Lake Trail soon enters a meadow and then crosses a floating bridge over a side stream. When the water level rises, the bridge floats up and then settles back into place when the water drops. The trail skirts the edge of private land to emerge on the paved road L.R. 55049 at 10.9 km (6.8 miles). Turn right past the gas station and food store, cross the bridge over Laurel Hill Creek and immediately turn right again on a fisherman's trail. This trail is informal and unmaintained but it goes all the way to the base of the dam. (Most fisherman's trails only go as far as the first place the fish bite.) Along the way you will see spruce and white pine in an evergreen plantation, large white oak, ironwood, beech, serviceberry, red oak, rhododendron, azalea and perhaps even someone fishing. When you reach the dam, cut left along the base, and make your way behind the beach to the concession stand. Turn left, and you are soon back to the beach parking area in which you left your car.

A longer hike in Roaring Run Natural Area on the other side of Laurel Hill is described in Hike 9.

11

Quebec Run Wild Area

Distance: 13.0 km (8.1 miles)
Time: 4½ hours
Rise: 315 meters (1,040 feet)
Highlights: Abandoned "gold mine"; mountain streams
Maps: USGS 7½' Bruceton Mills, Brownfield; State Forest Wild
  Area map

The Quebec Run Wild Area is a heavily forested section of land in Forbes State Forest on the eastern slope of Chestnut Ridge, just a bit north of the Mason-Dixon Line. Chestnut Ridge, like Laurel Ridge, is an anticline. Layers of rock have been gently folded to form a great arch. It helps to have the topmost layer a hard one, resistant to erosion. The hard upper layer of Chestnut Ridge is Pottsville sandstone. This stone is of great significance in Pennsylvania because all the commercial coal seams lie above it. There are a few traces of Devonian coal below but they are of interest primarily to geologists. Quebec Run Wild Area also contains Pennsylvania's only "gold mine". The geology is all wrong for a gold mine in Pennsylvania. Legend has it that raiding Confederate calvary robbed the gold from banks in southwestern Pennsylvania and buried it on Chestnut Ridge when it appeared they might not make it back to their own lines. People hunting for the gold after the Civil War dug the so-called mine. It is not known if any gold was ever recovered.

The trailhead for Quebec Run Wild Area is most easily reached from US 40 east of Uniontown. Turn south at the top of Chestnut Ridge on the Seaton Road, just east of the Mount Summit Inn. Follow the signs for Laurel Caverns but continue past the cavern turnoff. Bypass the road to Pondfield Fire Tower (which, by the way, commands a splendid view of Chestnut Ridge). At 6.5 miles from US 40, turn left on the Mud Pike (no sign but well named) for 1.3 miles more to the parking lot at the north end of the gated Quebec Road.

The hike starts off from the parking lot on the blue-blazed Miller Trail, which descends gently along a ridge between Mill Run and a nameless tributary to the west. Chestnut Ridge was named for the American chestnut, which sprouts abundantly along this trail. The chestnut was a versatile tree; in town its spreading branches provided shade, while in the forest it grew straight and tall for timber. Its beautiful wood was suitable for both rough and fine construction, and since it resisted rot, it was used for fence posts, too. When the tree was cut, the stump would resprout vigorously. The nuts provided food for both wildlife and humans. At the turn of the century the American chestnut comprised about half of the wood in the Appalachians from Maine to Georgia. These forests were decimated by a fungal blight (*Endothia parasitica*) which killed the above-ground portion of the trees. The fungus may have been introduced in a shipment of trees or logs from Europe. The roots were not affected, however; and today, some eighty years later, they continue to send up healthy shoots. Although some of these shoots grow large enough to bear nuts, they eventually contract the blight and die. Recently, though, a viral parasite that weakens *Endothia parasitica* was introduced. Perhaps, at long last, the tide is about to turn, and the American chestnut may once again cover the many flats, ridges and hollows that now bear only its name and the few stumps where life continues to linger underground.

Up Mill Run at 1.4 km (0.9 mile) you

View East from Chestnut Ridge

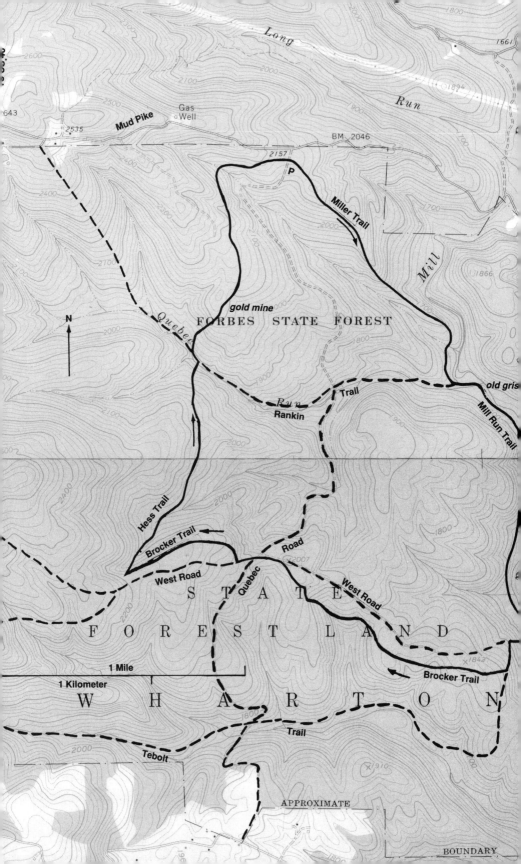

pass a mini-view; then cross a nameless tributary on stepping stones. The stream flows through a rhododendron thicket. A little farther along, the trail follows an old logging railroad grade.

Look for deer tracks in the mud. I found two sets, one full-sized, the other diminutive. The tracks were so fresh and sharp that I suspect the deer were moving down the trail ahead of me, just far enough ahead to keep out of sight.

At 2.1 km (1.3 miles) bear left on the Mill Run Trail at the junction with the Rankin Trail. The Miller Trail ends here. Trail signs are where you find them at Quebec Run. Some are spiked to trees while others are nailed to posts. Still others rest quietly on the ground. Shortly you must cross Quebec Run itself. It is too wide to jump, but a pile of logs a bit downstream served as a somewhat slippery bridge for me. In slightly lower water, you should be able to use the stepping stones or take off your boots and wade.

Next, you reach the edge of Mill Run itself, a formidable stream. A modular truss bridge of the Drexel design has been built across Mill Run at this spot. It connects with the Grist Mill Trail on the east side of Mill Run. To see the ruins of the old mill itself cross the bridge and turn right, downstream. The Grist Mill Trail takes you between the stone foundation and the mill race. Back on the west side of Mill Run, the Mill Run Trail continues downstream, sometimes right along Mill Run, and at other times out of sight of the stream. The old railroad grade is used whenever it is on the west side, but frequently it is on the east side. You cross many side streams, some small and some rather large. Turn right on the West Road at 4.6 km (2.9 miles) and start the long climb back up the flank of Chestnut Ridge. At 4.8 km

(3.0 miles) turn left on the Tebolt Trail and continue to climb, but more gently, as you follow it through a small meadow.

You reach the Brocker Trail at 5.1 km (3.2 miles) and turn right on it through a stand of larch or tamarack. At 5.7 km (3.6 miles) you cross the Tebolt Road. Continue ahead on the Brocker Trail, crossing a ravine and the traces of several old logging roads, to the Quebec road at 7.2 km (4.5 miles). Cross the Quebec Road and continue on the West Road. Soon, you turn right on the relocated Brocker Trail. Follow the Brocker Trail to its unsigned junction with the Hess Trail. Turn right on the Hess Trail, which takes you downhill on an old road along a stream. You cross this stream and then another one before descending into the valley of Quebec Run itself, which you cross at 10.4 km (6.5 miles). Immediately up the bank, turn left on the Rankin Trail and follow it around the bend to where the Hess Trail turns right uphill.

At the top of the hill the old "gold mine" diggings appear to the right of the trail, and just beyond there is a view to the east; cross a stream and continue climbing. At 12.4 km (7.8 miles), cross an old road and continue to the parking lot.

Backpacking is permitted in the Quebec Run Wild Area, but you should obtain a camping permit from the district forest office on the north side of PA 30, east of Laughlintown. The Rankin Trail, Tebolt Trail, and Quebec Road provide alternatives that could be used to either lengthen or shorten this hike. For a cool hike underground, you might visit Laurel Caverns.

The trails at Quebec Run Wild Area are scheduled to be modified in the next few years.

12

Bear Run Nature Reserve

Distance: 14.3 km (8.8 miles)
Time: 5¼ hours
Rise: 355 meters (1,160 feet)
Highlights: Wildflowers; mountain streams; views
Maps: USGS 7½' Mill Run; Bear Run Trail Map (frequently
available at trailhead and from Western Pennsylvania
Conservancy)

Normally, the Western Pennsylvania Conservancy transfers acquired lands to public ownership. There is one area, however, that the Conservancy chose to keep. This is the Bear Run Nature Reserve. The Conservancy has expanded the original tract surrounding Fallingwater, Frank Lloyd Wright's famous house, to 1,400 hectares (3,500 acres). The Reserve stretches from the banks of the Youghiogheny far up the western flank of Laurel Hill and encompasses most of the watersheds of both Laurel Run and Bear Run itself. Almost 32 kilometers (20 miles) of trails lace the reserve, which is open to nonmembers for both day hiking and overnight camping. Users of the backpack campsites should register at the parking lot. Reservations are required for the one group campsite (l0 or more campers).

This hike, which can be shortened in several ways, takes you on a grand tour of the trails at Bear Run, through dense woods, pine plantations, and rhododendron thickets, across fields and along mountain streams to a view of rafts and kayaks knocking the rocks out

of the lower Yough. The many rocks and wet areas call for hiking boots.

Bear Run Nature Reserve is on PA 381 about 4 miles north of Ohiopyle and 3.5 miles south of Mill Run. Drive in at the sign and park in the large lot behind the nature center. The hike begins at the far end of the parking lot.

Head into the pine plantation on the Wagon Trail. Almost immediately the Pine Trail takes off to the left, and very shortly the Arbutus Trail diverges to the right. In theory the Wagon Trail is blazed with orange rectangles, but the trail is wide and well-used and the blazing scarce. The Poetry Trail goes off to your right. The white pine along the Wagon Trail give way to red pine. After the Aspen Trail, which goes left, you come to spruce.

At 0.8 km (0.5 mile) the Wagon Trail comes to an end and you turn left on the Ridge Trail blazed with yellow spots. Rhododendron thickets and white oaks border the trail at this point. Shortly, you cross a bridge over Beaver Run, and the Arbutus Trail comes in from the right. Listen for the song of the wood thrush. Next, the white-blazed Rhododendron Trail goes off to the left. (One way to shorten this hike and avoid over 90 meters of climbing would be to take the Rhododendron and Snowbunny trails to the junction of the Laurel Run and Tulip Tree trails.) At l.0 km (0.6 mile) the Hemlock Trail goes off to the right. Other trees found along this section are red oak, tulip, black gum, chestnut oak, cucumber, black birch, red maple, and the much smaller striped maple. At l.7 km (1.1 miles) bear left where the Hemlock Trail comes back in from the right, and left again at l.9 km (1.2 miles) where the old road goes straight ahead.

Teaberry Trail comes in from the left at 2.0 km (1.3 miles). Along this section you can see sassafras and beech as well as mountain laurel. Backpack campsite 2 is found at 3.4 km (2.1 miles). At 3.8 km (2.4 miles) you reach a junction with the Rhododendron, Bear Run, and Tulip Tree Trails. Continue straight ahead on the Tulip Tree Trail, which is also blazed with yellow spots. In late May, look for the pink lady's slipper. At 4.l km (2.6 miles) watch the blazes as the Tulip Tree makes an obscure jog to the left near some large rocks. For the most part, the Tulip Tree Trail is fairly faint and requires careful attention, particularly at junctions with other old woods roads.

Soon the trail begins descending, and at 5.6 km (3.5 miles) you reach the junction with the Snowbunny Trail. This is your last chance to return to the parking lot without going around the large inholding of private land or walking back on the highway. Continue ahead on the white-blazed Laurel Run Trail, and another 0.4 km (0.25 mile) brings you to a crossing of Laurel Run itself and you follow along it until you reach the edge of a field. Turn left and pick up a new trail

that takes you down to PA 38l at 7.0 km (4.4 miles).

Cross the highway and continue downhill. Soon you turn left, cross Laurel Run, pass through a rhododendron tunnel, and climb into more open woods above the stream. Pass through the gates of two barbed wire fences and remember to close them behind you. The trail returns to the side of Laurel Run at the ruins of a dam. Just beyond, a spur trail leads right to a view of lower Laurel Glen before returning to the main trail. The trail then climbs away from Laurel Run, picks up an old road grade, emerges into the lower Yough gorge, and swings upstream, following the old road far above the river. At 9.5 km (5.9 miles) you reach a junction with the orange-blazed Saddle Trail which, if you take it, will shorten your hike but will also bypass the overlook on the Yough at the west end of the peninsula.

Just beyond this junction you pass campsite no. 4 to the right of the trail.

At l0.6 km (6.6 miles) the trail picks up a pole line. At times the trail follows an old quarry above the pole line. At ll.6 km (7.3 miles) however, you emerge at an overlook that makes it all worthwhile. You are 20 meters directly above the main line of the Baltimore and Ohio Railroad. You get a good view of the river at Dimple Rapids and can watch the kayaks and rafts dodging the many rocks. You probably heard the screams and shouts from below as you hiked the Peninsula Trail, but now you can actually see what is going on.

Back on the Peninsula Trail you traverse the slope for the next 0.9 km (0.6 mile) on a new trail cut by the Keystone Trails Association Trail Care team in 1988. At l2.4 km (7.8 miles) you reach the Daniel G. Paradise Memorial Overlook at the brink of an impressive cliff. Continuing on the Peninsula Trail climb to the edge of a field where you turn right and the Saddle Trail comes in from the left. At the far edge of the field, you can vary the walk back by turning left on the yellow-blazed Kinglet Trail or continuing on the Peninsula Trail. In either case, it is about 0.8 km (0.5 mile) back to PA 38l, just across from the entrance to the Bear Run parking lot.

As this hike uses less than half the trails in Bear Run Nature Reserve, there are plenty of opportunities for further hiking. As mentioned earlier, Fallingwater, the famous house designed by Frank Lloyd Wright, is near at hand, and well worth a visit.

To reach Fallingwater, turn south on PA 38l for half a mile, then turn right at the sign.

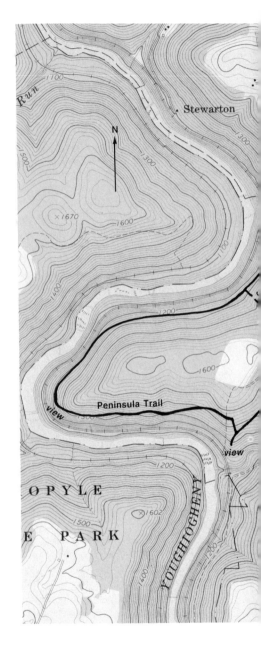

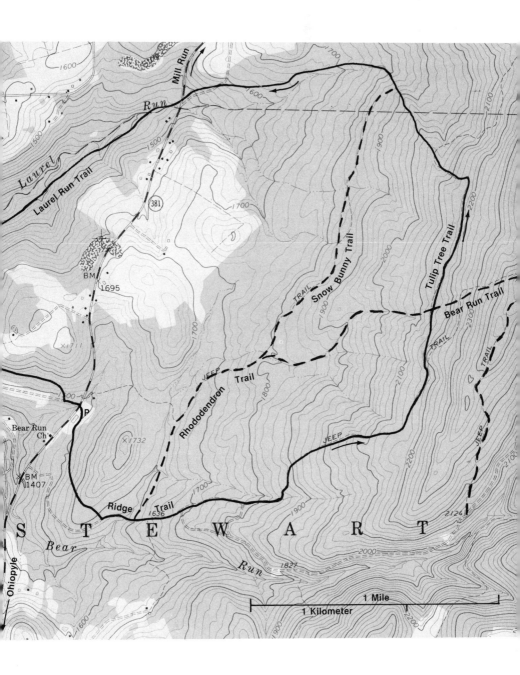

Mill Run

Laurel Run Trail

Laurel Run

381

BM 1695

×1711

Bear Run Ch.

× BM 1407

P

Snow Bunny Trail

TRAIL

Tulip Tree Trail

TRAIL

Bear Run Trail

TRAIL

JEEP

Rhododendron Trail

JEEP

JEEP

×1732

Ridge Trail

1636

S   T   E   W   A   R   T

Bear   Run

1827

Ohiopyle

2124

1 Mile

1 Kilometer

13

Maple Summit to Ohiopyle

Distance: 18.0 km (11.3 miles)
Time: 6¼ hrs
Rise: 520 meters (1,700 feet)
Highlight: Views
Maps: USGS 7½' Mill Run, Ohiopyle; Hikers Guide to the
Laurel Highlands Trail, maps 1 and 2; Laurel Ridge State
Park map

Laurel Ridge is a giant arch of gently folded rock; an anticline. Like Chestnut Ridge, its cap is composed of a layer of Pottsville sandstone which resists erosion. This sandstone lies under the Ohiopyle waterfall, then rises gently upwards—about 500 meters—to form Laurel Ridge. This is a modest anticline compared to some in the ridge-and-valley region to the east which appear to have exceeded 9,000 meters. Laurel Ridge has survived more or less intact, whereas the ridge-and-valley anticlines have been leveled by erosion.

The Youghiogheny River has cut a water gap through Laurel Ridge, making this southernmost section of the Laurel Highlands Trail one of the most scenic. For much of its length the top of Laurel Ridge is broad and relatively flat, making views and overlooks rare. The section between Ohiopyle and Maple Summit also contains one of the longest climbs on the Laurel Highlands Trail. While this hike is arranged so that you go down this hill, the north flank of Youghiogheny Gorge still requires several steep climbs.

To do this hike you need a car shuttle, or preferably a drop-off service. At the time of this writing, however, none of the outfitters at Ohiopyle was interested in providing this service for hikers. Leave one car in a lot in Ohiopyle and drive north on PA 381 in the other car. At 1.9 miles north of the bridge, turn right and drive up the flank of Laurel Ridge. After 4.0 miles more, turn right again. It is another 1.8 miles to the obscure trail crossing. There is no parking at the crossing, but there is a game commission parking lot on the left, just 0.1 mile farther, and there is a side trail to the Laurel Highlands Trail from the lot. Overnight parking is not permitted at the game commission lot. There are shelters on this section of the trail, so this hike could be turned into a two-day backpack if you can make drop-off arrangements. Whether you do this as a day hike or as a backpack, hiking boots are strongly recommended.

As you head south along the yellow-blazed Laurel Highlands Trail, the first landmark you see is milepost 11 at 0.6 km (0.4 mile) from the Maple Summit

Trail Shelter

Road. Despite the substantial split log bridges at the many wet spots there is still a good deal of water on this section of trail. At 1.5 km (0.9 mile) you cross Little Glade Run and begin a gentle climb towards the western edge of Laurel Hill. After passing some big rocks, you reach milepost 10. Pass along the base of a small cliff on your right, and at 2.8 km (1.8 miles) cross a jeep road in a cleared swath. This road appears to service several natural gas wells. Anticlines like Laurel Ridge are textbook traps for oil and gas. Alex Run is crossed at 3.7 km (2.3 miles), and shortly you reach milepost 9. Approach the edge of Laurel Ridge where the "Hiker's Guide to Laurel Highlands Trail" indicates a view to the west. When I finally got to see this view it was disappointing.

The trail continues close to the western edge, past milepost 8. At 6.2 km (3.9 miles) there are several obvious side trails out to more views. These

views are much better than the previous one as you can see Laurel Hill dropping away towards the Youghiogheny.

Start down the great descent into the Youghiogheny Gorge. Twice you cross another jeep road that leads to some natural gas wells. At 7.0 km (4.4 miles) bear right on an old road and pass milepost 7. There is a view over Camp Run Ravine as you continue to descend. Shortly you pass a white-blazed boundary between State Game Land No. 111 and Ohiopyle State Park.

A side trail goes left to the Camp Run shelters at 8.1 km (5.0 miles). If you've never seen a Laurel Highlands Trail shelter, take the time to inspect one. The built-in fireplace provides good heat. There is a well here for drinking water and also pit toilets, including one for the handicapped.

Back on the Laurel Highlands Trail, at the bottom of the great descent, there is a meadow. At 8.5 km (5.3 miles), cross a jeep road and Lick Run to milepost 6.

The trail continues in and out of meadows to 9.5 km (5.9 miles) where you cross a nameless stream. This is followed by a good stiff climb that continues past milepost 5. Follow along the hillside high above the Yough, which affords occasional views of the other side of the gorge, and at 11.8 km (7.4 miles) you reach milepost 4 above the large bend in the Yough that encloses the Flats. There is a fair amount of open meadow along this section. At 12.5 km (7.8 miles) cross Rock Spring Run and begin another climb that continues almost to milepost 3.

The Laurel Highlands Trail has saved the best for last. At 14.5 km (9.1 miles) you come to the edge of cliffs with spectacular views of the Yough and spectacular drops to the rocks below.

Be careful. There are no guard rails. From here the trail leads downward until it is just above the Baltimore and Ohio tracks. A giant boulder is passed at 16.5 km (10.3 miles), then milepost 1. Cross Sheepskin Run and then another run. A trail at 17.2 km (10.8 miles) leads right to the hiker parking lot.

Shortly the Laurel Highlands Trail bears left off an old road, descends, and turns right onto the jeep road along the Baltimore and Ohio tracks. Please sign the trail register. Maintenance of the Laurel Highlands Trail depends on the level of usage. Continue into the outskirts of Ohiopyle; 18.0 km (11.3 miles) brings you to PA 381.

There are other hikes at Ohiopyle State Park and nearby Bear Run Nature Reserve. See Hikes 1, 6, 12 and 14.

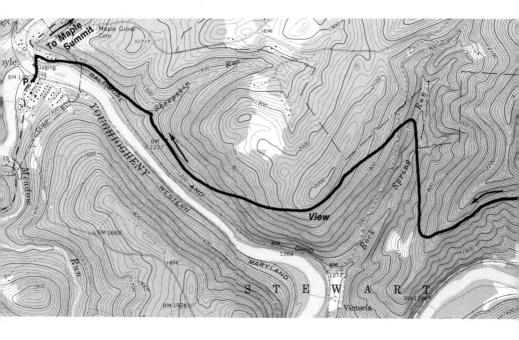

Baughman's Rock and Sugarloaf Knob

Distance: 14.6 km (9.0 miles)
Time: 5 hours
Rise: 460 meters (1510 feet)
Highlights: Views of Youghiogheny River and Sugarloaf Knob
Maps: USGS 7½' Ohiopyle; state park map

This hike takes you up the steep southern side of the Youghiogheny Gorge to a natural overlook called Baughman's (pronounced Bachman's) Rock and then through meadows around Sugarloaf Knob, a distinctively shaped high point. It is a real circuit hike that doesn't retrace any trail. Despite its length the entire hike is within the borders of Ohiopyle State Park and parallels the paved Ohiopyle to Confluence Road (L.R. 26116). To divide the hike into two half-day car shuttle hikes, use the Sugarloaf snowmobile parking area. Rocks and wet spots call for hiking boots and there is some poison ivy along the trail.

The hike begins just outside the village of Ohiopyle at the middle Yough takeout and trailhead. From PA 381 turn east next to Falls Market (formerly Holt's Department Store), bear left just beyond the old Western Maryland railroad station and continue to the far end of the parking lot.

At the far end the Western Maryland grade is blocked by posts and both the Baughman and Sugarloaf trails begin. Follow the red-blazed Baughman Trail as it climbs away from the railroad grade. After a particularly steep pitch

you reach an old road that comes from the end of a street in Ohiopyle. Turn left and continue climbing at a more gradual rate, passing a patch of rhododendrons. At 1.0 km (0.6 mile) bear right on another old road just beyond a big rock to the left. Three more old roads to the left are passed as you continue to climb. The trail levels off briefly, but climbs again by the time you reach a small clearing at 2.4 km (1.5 miles). Avoid the obvious old road ahead and turn sharply to the left. Along this stretch the trail is also marked with faded orange arrows painted on white boards. The trees along the trail here were completely defoliated by gypsy moth caterpillars in 1989.

Soon the trail comes within sight of the paved road (L.R. 26116) and at 3.3 km (2.1 miles) you reach the parking lot for Baughman's Rock. Turn left for a vista of Baughman Hollow, the flats inside the bend of the Youghiogheny and Laurel Ridge beyond.

Continuing beyond Baughman's Rock keep left. The real Baughman Trail leads through the formation of large rocks of which Baughman Rock is a part. The paved road slowly forces the

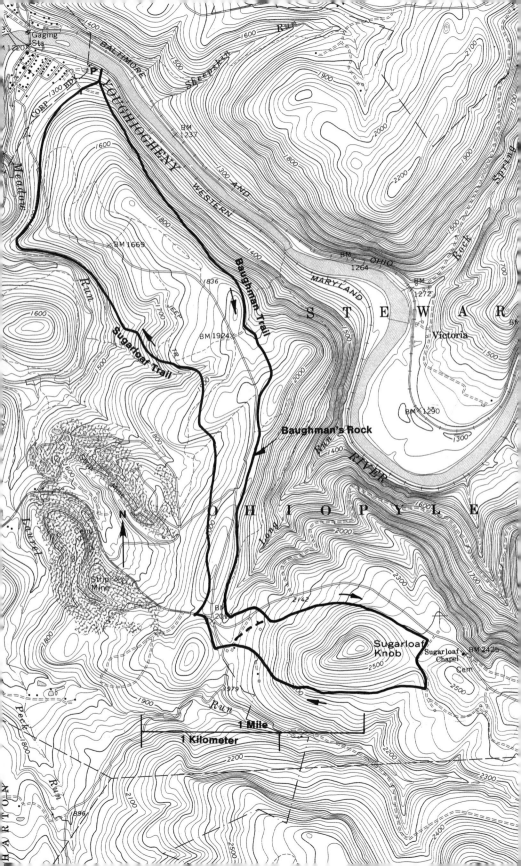

Baughman Trail

trail over the edge to descend a little below the rim where it continues on a succession of old roads.

Sometimes in such thick vegetation you may hear a large animal go crashing through the brush. It comes to a halt, still entirely out of sight. Now you hear a succession of snorts accompanied by hoof stomps. What is it? A bear? A wild boar? No, it's just a deer. If the deer hears you but can't get wind of you, it can't figure out what you are. It's hard to believe that deer can make such undeerlike noises but they do.

Cross Long Run on a split log bridge and climb back to the paved road which you cross at 5.0 km (3.1 miles). Just beyond, there is a junction with the "Loop Return" which is part of the Sugarloaf Knob snowmobile trail system. You could truncate the hike at this point by turning right and following the Loop Return to the Sugarloaf Trail junction at 8.5 km (5.3 miles). However, this hike follows the Baughman Trail, which turns left and climbs into open meadows to the north of Sugarloaf Knob. In season these meadows are brilliant with goldenrod. The snowmobile trails are mowed about three meters wide. At 5.3 km (3.3 miles) a trail goes left to the paved road, which is never far away. Continue climbing past Sugarloaf Knob to the snowmobile parking lot, the end of the Baughman Rock Trail, and a junction with the Sugarloaf Trail.

Bluebird houses have been installed in the surrounding meadows, so in the spring and summer look for these birds which Thoreau said carry the sky on their backs.

Turn right on the Sugarloaf Trail and follow it along a lane between two meadows to a height of land. Beyond, the trail swings left and then right as it enters woods along the edge of the meadows. Snowmobiles pay a license fee, part of which is used to pay for the construction and maintenance of snowmobile trails. Hence the excellent condition of the trails around Sugarloaf.

At 8.0 km (5.0 miles) you reach the corner of another meadow and shortly pass a large white pine. The junction with the "Loop Return" is reached at 8.5 km (5.3 miles), and just beyond you cross a gravel road. The snowmobile trail is blocked with a large post that says "NO VEHICLES", but the post is equipped with handles. In winter it can be unlocked and lifted out to permit the passage of snow machines.

At 8.9 km (5.5 miles) the Sugarloaf Trail jogs left 150 meters on another gravel road before reentering the woods. The trail beyond this point is marked with occasional orange blazes. It climbs gently back to the edge of the paved road before turning away and pursuing a more independent route. At 10 km (6.2 miles), cross a jeep road and at 10.3 km (6.4 miles) bear right on an old woods road which is followed for the rest of the hike. The trail follows a small run, but at 11.0 km (6.8 miles) continue on a bit of new trail that briefly avoids the old woods road.

At 11.6 km (7.2 miles) pass a spring to the right and just beyond go straight ahead, avoiding an old switchback to the right. The Sugarloaf Trail then levels off and continues along the contour on the steep mountainside.

At 13.6 km (8.5 miles) cross the paved road for the last time and continue along Sugarloaf Trail as it passes above the village of Ohiopyle. Jog left across a jeep road at 14.3 km (8.9 miles) and descend to the middle Yough parking lot.

Other hiking opportunities at Ohiopyle State Park are hikes 1, 6 and 13. In addition, there is a small network of trails along Meadow Run, just north of the park office, that are known for spring wildflowers.

15

New Florence Game Lands

Distance: 16.9 km (10.5 miles)
Time: 5 hours
Rise: 510 meters (1,680 feet)
Highlights: Laurel Highlands Trail, iron furnace
Maps: USGS 7½' Rachel Wood; Hiker's Guide to the Laurel
  Highlands Trail, map 11

In the western part of the state there are over 100,000 hectares (247,000 acres) of state game lands. They are the most abundant type of public lands, second only to the lands of the Allegheny National Forest, yet these lands have few marked trails. The Laurel Highlands Trail traverses game lands 111 and 42 while the Baker Trail passes through game lands 24, 283 and 74. Since the Pennsylvania Game Commission is supported primarily by hunting license fees, you can understand why it tries to serve hunters rather than hikers.

This hike is located in the largest of four tracts comprising State Game Land No. 42. This tract is located on the west flank of Laurel Hill, above the small town of New Florence.

You will see evidence of past industrial activity on Laurel Hill. It hasn't always been as wild as it is today.

The trailhead is the game commission parking lot at the end of the road from New Florence. New Florence is 7.6 miles south of US 22 on PA 711. At the south edge of town turn east on Furnace Lane. There is a State Game Land sign at this junction. Continue straight ahead at a stop sign 0.8 mile from PA 711. Turn right at 1.0 mile and pass a large charcoal iron furnace. The parking lot and end of the road are at 1.7 miles. Due to the length of this hike, hiking boots are the choice.

To start the hike, squeeze around the gate and proceed to a cluster of storage buildings. Just beyond the large garage turn left, cross a bridge over Baldwin Creek and start up the gravel management road. The road is marked with occasional orange diamonds showing this road is a snowmobile trail in season (15 January to 15 April). Soon you reach a small meadow on your right but avoid a road to your left that dead ends at some game food plots. At 0.8 km (0.5 mile) you reach the corner of a clear-cut made in 1978. This clear-cut has certainly greened up.

At 1.6 km (1.0 mile) avoid a road to the right which leads uphill to some more recent clear-cuts. You reach the first of a series of switchbacks at 2.4 km (1.5 miles). There are five switchbacks in all as you continue to make your way up the flank of Laurel Hill.

At 3.8 km (2.3 miles) the climbing eases off but you enter a region of gypsy moth damage centered around a selective timber cut of recent vintage. Some healthy trees have been left to seed in a new generation of forest.

A mysterious fenced-in structure is passed at 4.5 km (2.8 miles). A grassy swath containing a buried electric cable follows the management road. Most likely this is just another gas well. At 5.7 km (3.6 miles) there is an active (1989) logging road to the left. Turn left at 6.2 km (3.8 miles) on a swath of a major pipeline. After just 100 meters, turn right on the yellow-blazed Laurel Highlands Trail which follows another major pipeline at this point.

Along this section the Laurel Highlands Trail is out in the open on the service road along the pipeline. The adjacent portion of the game lands is a wildlife refuge. Not only is hunting prohibited within the refuge but the hiking trail has also been excluded. The yellow blazes are on wooden posts along the border of the pipeline swath. There is a recent clear-cut on the left, which permits a view over the eastern flank of Laurel Ridge.

At 8.1 km (5.0 miles) another management road comes in from the right, and the Laurel Highlands Trail bears right into the woods. Mountain laurel proliferates along this section, even approaching central Pennsylvania

Baldwin Iron Furnace

densities. There is also a stand of black gum trees that turn the woods red in early fall. At 9.4 km (5.8 miles) you pass milepost 60.

At 9.8 km (6.1 miles) turn right on another management road. At the time of my hike this road was a muddy mess due to logging at the Rachel Wood Game Preserve. Follow the road to the corner of this fenced-off private game preserve at 11.2 km (6.9 miles). There is a gate here for the logging trucks. From this point you can see that what foresters call site conversion is in progress. Not only have large areas been clear-cut but the slash has been burned. Conversion of the woods to meadows should increase the carrying capacity for the game animals, some of them exotic, stocked at Rachel Wood.

Turn left along the fence and follow the management road, which is its old grassy self from here on. As soon as the logging is completed, the rest of this road should revert to grass. At 11.6 km (7.2 miles) avoid an old road to the right. Your way continues down, steeply at times, but also leveling off from time to time.

Pass an old selective cut where at one point, the bedrock itself outcrops in the road. At 13.8 km (8.6 miles) bear left and cross a natural gas pipeline. Continue down, passing game food plots. Switchback sharply to the right and cross a bridge over Shannon Run. The stream is bordered with hemlock and rhododendron.

At 14.8 km (9.2 miles) turn left on another management road. Rhododendron grows along this road as you approach Baldwin Creek, making this section particularly attractive. Ignore a road to the left and pass Baldwin Iron Furnace to the right, evidence of past industrial activity. A small pond can be seen to the right at 16.4 km (10.2 miles) and you soon pass an old mine or quarry on the left.

Pass a road from the right and reach the game commission storage buildings at 16.7 km (10.4 miles). Continue ahead and you are soon back at your car.

Other nearby hiking opportunities are Conemaugh Gorge (Hike 8) and Charles F. Lewis Natural Area (Hike 2).

Allegheny
National Forest

16

Anders Tract Natural Area

Distance: 3.2 km (2.0 miles)
Time: 1½ hours
Rise: 58 meters (190 feet)
Highlight: Old growth white pines
Map: USGS 7½' Youngsville

Just west of Warren, near the town of Ir-vine, lies a small tract of old growth white pine along Anders Run. The Western Pennsylvania Conservancy, with help from the Northern Allegheny Conservation Association, De Frees Family Foundation and National Forge Company, bought this tract and subsequently transferred the 39 hectares (100 acres) to Cornplanter State Forest.

The Anders Tract is conveniently close to the Allegheny River and must have been cut very early in the nineteenth century. The old growth white pine and hemlock are estimated to be 170 years old. The largest pines are more than a meter in diameter and up to 36 meters tall. Climax vegetation in this part of Penns Woods is probably a mixture of hemlock and northern hardwoods such as beech. At Cook Forest (Hike 23) and Hearts Content (Hike 17) you can see that the old white pine are dying and the climax forest is taking over. The Anders Tract is relatively young and its pines should be with us for a couple of centuries to come. The state foresters

Roots

have been busy establishing trails in their newly-acquired natural area.

To reach the trailhead from US 6 west of Warren turn south on US 62 and, in just 0.2 mile, turn right for Buckaloons. Continue past Buckaloons and the N.E. Forest Experiment Station. After 0.9 mile, turn left on the paved Dunns Eddy River Road. Drive south for 1.0 mile and park in the large area on the left side of the road. Foot bridges have been built across Anders Run, so you can manage this hike with walking shoes.

To start the hike, cross the paved road with care as it is on a curve. Head up an obvious woods road and in just a few steps turn left on a trail which is marked with yellow diamonds; this trail parallels the dirt road along Anders Run. After crossing two small streams you reach the loop trail junction at 0.4 km (0.3 mile). Continue ahead. At 0.7 km (0.4 mile) you pass among some large boulders and large white pines. These are the trees that first attracted large-scale logging to Pennsylvania. Other trees growing here are white oak, beech, hemlock and ash.

Next, jog right across a woods road and proceed to 1.0 km (0.7 mile) where

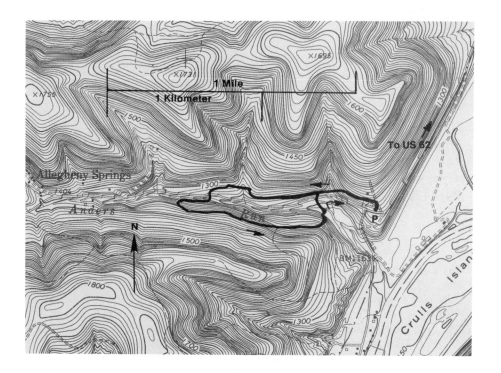

you turn left on a logging road and cross a stream by means of a culvert. After 100 meters bear left on the trail and proceed to a crossing of the dirt road along Anders Run. Then cross Anders Run and head upstream.

Soon you climb above the run among some large hemlocks. At the top of the slope you turn left and follow the trail downstream along the break in the slope. At 1.8 km (1.1 miles) the trail switchbacks down a slope. Shortly beyond, you cross a stream, climb a bank on stone steps and turn left. At 2.2 km (1.3 miles) you pass what appears to be

the largest white pine along the trail.

Descend and cross Anders Run on another foot bridge at 2.4 km (1.5 miles). On the far side, turn left and proceed upstream among some large hemlocks. After 250 meters, turn away from the stream, cross the dirt road and arrive at the loop trail junction at 2.8 km (1.8 miles). Turn right and retrace your steps to your car.

Other hiking opportunities near the Anders Tract are Slater Run (Hike 21), Hearts Content (Hike 17), Tom Run (Hike 19), Hickory Creek Trail (Hike 29) and Chapman State Park (Hike 25).

17

Hearts Content Scenic Area

Distance: 1.8 km (1.1 miles)
Time: ¾ hour
Rise: 35 meters (110 feet)
Highlights: Virgin timber, log display, wheelchair accessible
  in part
Maps: USGS 7½' Cherry Grove, Cobham

White pine was the most valuable tree growing in Penn's Woods during the nineteenth century logging era. But white pine doesn't belong to the region's climax vegetation. It is, instead, an opportunistic tree that grows in large stands following some disaster to the mature forest, such as a windstorm or fire. The great stands of white pine that the nineteenth century loggers exploited in Pennsylvania are attributed to the fires of 1644. By then there were colonists settled along the Atlantic Coast. They wrote home all summer about the poor air quality as the smoke from many forest fires rolled out of the interior.

This white pine made Pennsylvania first in timber production after the Civil War. Production continued to rise until late in the nineteenth century. But by then several western states had passes Pennsylvania in output of timber.

At Hearts Content a small tract of white pine has been preserved much as the loggers found it. Unlike many other small tracts of virgin lumber in Pennsylvania the circumstances are well known. In 1922 the firm of Wheeler and Dusenbury donated 8 hectares (20 acres) to the government. In 1931 another 40 hectares (100 acres) were

purchased by the federal government, bringing the Hearts Content Scenic Area to its present size.

An interpretive audiotape for Hearts Content can be checked out at the Bradford and Warren Forest Service offices. In summer the tape is also available from the campground host at Hearts Content Campground.

The trailhead for this hike is the Hearts Content picnic area, and the directions for reaching it are the same as for Hickory Creek (Hike 29). The Tom Run Hike (Hike 19) also leaves from the same parking area but now you want the obvious trail that leads to the virgin timber. An interpretive sign at the trailhead illustrates the history of the scenic area.

You come immediately to a marker that proclaims Hearts Content a registered Natural Landmark. The first part of the trail is smooth, compacted limestone for wheelchairs and strollers. Bear right past a dead pine. Many of the white pines are dead or dying. Also, many of the beech are dying of beech bark disease complex. In the parlance of foresters, the stand is "over mature," and we are watching the pines being replaced by shade-tolerant hemlocks. Already many of these hemlocks are very large

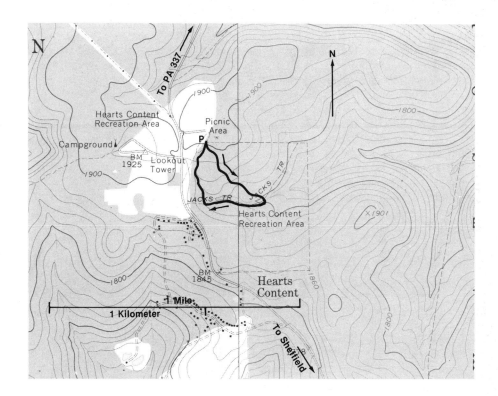

N

N

To PA 337

1900
1900

Hearts Content
Recreation Area

Picnic
Area

P

Campground

BM
1925

Lookout
Tower

1900

JACKS TR

JACKS TR

Hearts Content
Recreation Area

1800

X 1901

1800

1 Mile

1 Kilometer

BM
1845

Hearts
Content

1800

To Sheffield

trees in their own right. If left to itself, this forest would become a mixture of hemlock, birch and red maple.

Soon you reach a small fenced-in area. This is a deer enclosure area and it is intended to keep our overabundant deer herd from browsing here. You can see a great many more plants, shrubs and small trees growing within the fence than outside where the deer can eat them. These differences are now profound.

The wheelchair path turns right at this point. Continue on the well-defined gravel path.

At 0.6 km (0.4 mile) you reach a memorial to the Wheelers and Dusen-

burys, who ran their logging business for over a century. Immediately behind the memorial are several springs that constitute the source of the West Branch of Tionesta Creek. All about you are large white pines. Many companies cut pines this size and sawed them into standard-size timbers, and boards. Wheeler and Dusenbury specialized in long timbers. Their mill at Endeavor could cut logs up to 30 meters long. These long logs were primarily used as bridge timbers, but earlier in the century they had been used for masts and spars on sailing ships.

Such logs could not be loaded onto a single log car. Unless two steam-powered log loaders were available, they had to be loaded by hand. Wheeler and Dusenbury were still supplying such

Virgin Timber

special timbers when most of the rest of Penn's Woods had been cut over.

Beyond the memorial, you cross the headwaters of the West Branch and head back upstream. Other trees growing here are red maple, yellow birch, black birch, black cherry and white ash. At 1.3 km (0.8 miles) you turn right again, and at 1.7 km (1.1 miles), after passing another deer enclosure, you reach another junction with the wheelchair accessible trail. Continue on the compacted limestone surface and you will soon be back at the parking lot.

From the parking lot take a short trail north to a shelter housing a white pine timber squared by hand. Before railroads and steam-powered sawmills were built in all corners of the state, the only way to get timber to market was to raft it down the rivers leading to the Allegheny and Ohio. In those days, timbers were squared by hand and rafted as far as Cincinnati, Ohio, and Louisville, Kentucky.

18

Minister Creek Trail

Distance: 10.2 km (6.3 miles)
Time: 4 hours
Rise: 315 meters (1030 feet)
Highlights: View; cliffs and mountain stream
Maps: USGS 7½' Mayburg, Cherry Grove; Map 7 in Hiker's
  Guide to Allegheny National Forest

Minister Creek is probably the most famous of all the foot trails in Allegheny National Forest, and justly so. It has cliffs, big rocks, beautiful streams, part of the North Country National Scenic Trail as well as a natural overlook across Minister Valley. When sunlight dapples the forest floor on a day in early fall or wildflowers are in bloom on a spring day, this is one of the best trails to hike in all of Penns Woods. The Minister Creek Trail has long had a reputation for overuse but on my hike I found no evidence of overuse. Indeed I didn't meet anybody at all, but then it was a weekday. Minister Creek is shorter than generally advertised and although there are many exposed roots in the footway you should be able to negotiate it with good walking shoes. If you elect to backpack this trail, you will, of course, need hiking boots.

The trailhead for Minister Creek Trail is on PA 666 between the villages of Truemans and Porkey, 14.7 miles southwest of Sheffield. The parking area is just across the road from the Minister Creek campground.

To start the hike, cross PA 666 and

bear left. Then turn right and follow the 5"x7" white plastic blazes up an old grade.These blazes are strips of white plastic that are nailed to the trees with aluminum nails. When vandals discover how easy these strips are to remove, you will have to follow the trail by the remaining nail holes.

Bear right on forest road 537 at 200 meters. This road is closed to traffic. Note the trees growing on top of a boulder to the right of the trail. Next, avoid a grade to the left and then pass an old oil well also on the left. Continue on the trail at the end of the road and at 900 meters you reach the loop junction. Bear right downhill, passing some large boulders, and turn left on an old logging railroad grade at the bottom of the hill. Next, bear right off the old grade and cross Minister Creek on a bridge at 1.4 km (0.9 mile).

Beyond the creek the trail climbs gently but is soon out of sight of the creek. Large sandstone boulders can be seen above the trail. At 2.6 km (1.6 miles) a yellow-blazed side trail goes left down a pipeline to Deerlick Camp, about 800 meters from the main trail. A

small stream is crossed at 2.8 km (1.7 miles) and then the trail makes its way among more sandstone boulders. Trees along this section are black cherry, birch, maple and beech. Frequently the footway seems to consist entirely of beech roots.

Another small stream is crossed just before reaching the North Country Trail at 4.2 km (2.6 miles). Turn left on the

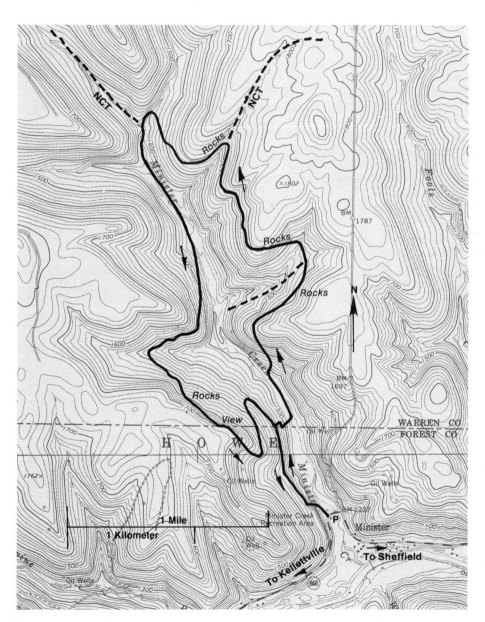

View over Minister Valley

white "eye" blazed North Country Trail and follow it down the hillside on an old road grade. At 4.6 km (2.9 miles) you pass a spring.

Note the old apple trees along the trail before you reach Triple Fork Camp at 4.9 km (3.0 miles). Here you cross two of the forks of Minister Creek on log bridges.

Just after the second bridge the North Country Trail turns right but you continue ahead on the blue-blazed Minister Creek Trail. At 5.4 km (3.3 miles) cross the third fork again on a two-log bridge. Soon the trail follows along the bank of the creek but at 5.8 km (3.4 miles) it climbs away from the creek before crossing another side stream. Head up a side valley and at 7.1 km (4.4 miles) turn sharply left and cross this stream. Beyond, the trail climbs and soon passes among more giant boulders. At 7.7 km (4.8 miles) you reach the base of cliffs of the Pottsville sandstone (note the layers of conglomerate), which are the source of all the giant boulders. The trail continues along the base of the cliffs, passing under overhangs and at one point traversing a narrow cleft behind a detached portion of the cliff. The top of the hill is reached at 8.0 km (5.0 miles) by means of a break in the cliffs. Minister Valley Overlook from the brink of the cliffs is just beyond. From the overlook you can look up and across Minister Valley.

Beyond, the trail descends through a couple of rock shelters to reach the loop junction at 9.3 km (5.8 miles). Then retrace your steps to your car on PA 666.

Additional hiking opportunities at Minister Creek would depend on following the North Country Trail either to the east or to the west.

19

Tom Run

Distance: 6.4 km (4.0 miles)
Time: 2 hours
Rise: 120 meters (400 feet)
Highlights: Mountain stream; Tanbark Trail; logging railroad
  grades
Maps: USGS 7½' Cherry Grove, Cobham

Within Allegheny National Forest the Tanbark Trail, which once stretched from Tionesta Scenic Area to US 62, used to be second in length only to the North Country Trail. The original or southern route of the North Country Trail crossed some private land within Allegheny National Forest. When the owners began to have second thoughts about the North Country Trail, the Forest Service simply abandoned the original route. The North Country Trail was relocated on the Tanbark Trail, reducing the Tanbark Trail to a fourteen kilometer (8.7 miles) section from near Dunham Siding to US 62. Nevertheless, the Tanbark passes through or near some of the most beautiful parts of Allegheny National Forest.

This hike uses part of the Tanbark Trail near Hearts Content Scenic Area and old logging railroad grades of Wheeler and Dusenbury that have been cleared for cross country ski trails to make a loop through the valley of Tom Run and the uppermost part of the West Branch of Tionesta Creek. Ordinary walking shoes should do for this hike as the crossings of Tom Run have been eliminated.

The trailhead is the picnic area at Hearts Content Scenic Area, the same as for Hike 17. If space permits, you can park in the picnic area lot, which has some shade around the edges, or use the large lot next door for Hickory Creek Trail (Hike 29). Avoid the obvious trail that leads to the virgin timber. Instead follow a trail to the left which is marked with 4"x4" blue plastic diamonds nailed to the trees. The cross country ski trail parallels the northern boundary of the Hearts Content Scenic Area and descends gently.

At 0.8 km (0.5 mile) turn left on the Tanbark Trail which is still marked with blue "eye" blazes. Follow the Tanbark over a low ridge and down the north slope.

At the bottom of the hill at 1.8 km (1.1 miles) turn right on Tom Run Trail which is again marked with blue diamonds. The trail is a logging railroad grade and you follow it across a small meadow. You can recognize that you are following an old railroad grade by the parallel depressions that cross the grade where the ties rotted in place. Indeed, in some wet places you can actually see the old ties themselves. They weren't squared or creosoted. They were just lengths of locally grown trees.

At some spots the grade tunnels through the hemlocks and at others it crosses open meadows. At one point in a meadow a family of grouse flushed, the chicks heading off in one direction, the hen in the other. The hen circled back, displaying her "broken wing" and cheeping piteously as she tried to draw me away from her chicks. Soon the

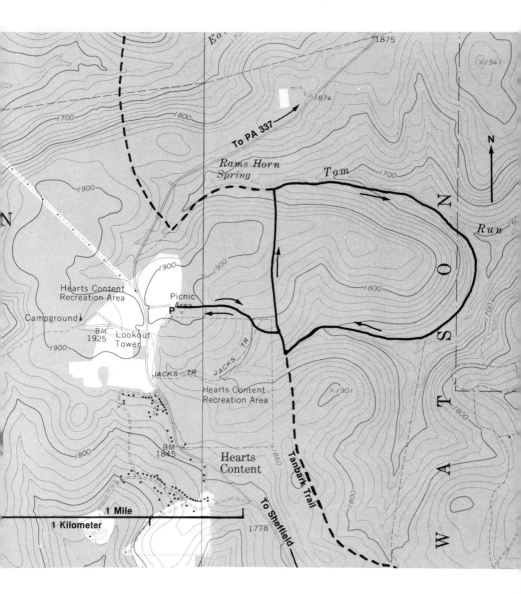

White Pine

wing healed miraculously and she circled around me to collect her brood.

At 3.0 km (1.9 miles) bear right on a relocation which avoids a pair of crossings of Tom Run. Note that some of the green blazes have turned blue.

At 3.3 km (2.1 miles) you pass a marker nailed to a tree which indicates you are crossing into State Game Land 29. A faint trail diverges to the left at 3.6 km (2.2 miles) but stick to the old railroad grade and begin the gentle climb back to the plateau. What a joy it would be to ski these trails! Your first sight of the West Branch near 4.3 km (2.7 miles) confirms that you are now walking upstream.

By the time you reach a junction with a red-blazed ski trail at 4.6 km (2.9 miles) you have recrossed onto national forest land. Keep right on a trail marked with both red and green diamonds. Near 5.0 km (3.1 miles) leave the railroad grade long enough to cross a small side stream on a bridge. The railroad bridge is long gone although elsewhere in this valley traces of old bridges still remain. Follow the green blazes when they diverge to the right. Soon you cross the Tanbark Trail and then retrace your steps along the green-blazed cross country ski trail to the picnic area and your car.

Additional hiking opportunities at Hearts Content are Hickory Creek Trail (Hike 29), Hearts Content Scenic Area (Hike 17) and Slater Run, which also uses the Tanbark Trail (Hike 21).

20

Clear Creek State Park

Distance: 8.3 km (5.2 miles)
Time: 3¼ hours
Rise: 270 meters (880 feet)
Highlights: Evergreen plantations; pileated woodpeckers
Maps: USGS 7½' Sigel; state park trail map

Clear Creek is a small state park just across the Clarion River from Allegheny National Forest. There are about 24 kilometers (15 miles) of trails in this park of only 485 hectares (1,200 acres). The park occupies the valley of Clear Creek between PA 949 and the Clarion. Many of the 17 trails used to cross Clear Creek on footbridges, but heavy rains on 9 June 1981 took out most of these bridges. This hike is designed to make use of the bridges that survive. You'll traverse the camping area in the park, so observe the prohibition on pets in that area. Despite some rocks and a few wet areas, good walking shoes should be adequate.

Clear Creek State Park is on PA 949, and the trailhead at the Beach House parking area is 3.9 miles from the junction with PA 36 in Sigel, which in turn is about 7 miles north of exit 13 on I-80 in Brookville. The hike starts on the Clear Creek Trail which you will find in the far left hand corner of the parking lot to the left of the water pump. This trail, like all those in the park, is marked with white, diamond-shaped blazes. Double blazes are used to mark turns and triple blazes to mark intersections and ends of trails.

Bear left almost immediately at a side trail that leads to the beach. Continue through a Norway spruce plantation with occasional aspen; witch hazel is also found along the trail, and at one place you pass a serviceberry that has grown to the size of a small tree.

Cross the Phyllis Run Trail, and shortly after that, the Ridge Trail diverges to the left. The trail then passes through a rhododendron thicket. Note the association between this shrub and the many spring seeps. Next, pass the Big Coon Trail and the Little Coon Trail, both of which descend toward Clear Creek. Black cherry is found along this section of the trail, and at another spot you see a large sandstone boulder on its leisurely way to the creek below.

At 1.3 km (0.8 mile) you arrive at the top of a steep bank above the creek, adorned with a white pine tree; turn left on an old railroad grade. This may be the old Frazier Railroad that served two steam-powered sawmills further up Clear Creek valley in the 1860s. It is not known whether the Frazier Railroad even had a locomotive; it could have used horses. There was no connecting railroad along the Clarion at that time, so the lumber must have been floated downstream on rafts or flatboats.

Immediately beyond, cross the pipeline swath that cuts across the valley. Pass a walk-in picnic area, and at 1.5 km (0.9 mile) cross Sawmill Run and continue on the old tram road.

The Sawmill Trail comes in from the left at 1.7 km (1.1 miles). A bit beyond, a piped spring comes out from underneath the trail.

One of the largest birds you may see in these woods is the pileated woodpecker. Next to the extraordinarily rare ivory-billed woodpecker, this crow-sized bird is the largest woodpecker in the world. Its presence is usually revealed by oval holes chiseled up to eight inches deep into trees. Its flight is swooping and reveals large white underwing patches. The call is like that of a

flicker but louder, deeper and woodier. The holes it makes in search of ants and grubs do not kill the trees, and its radical surgery may actually save the tree from these parasites.

At 2.0 km (1.3 miles) keep left at a junction with the Oxshoe Trail which diverges to the right, and at 2.4 km (1.5 miles) bear right on the gravel road in the campground. In traversing the campground you pass drinking water and cross Clear Creek on the road bridge. The Clarion River is on your left, and some benches are provided for enjoying the view.

At 2.9 km (1.8 miles) turn left on a paved road. Soon the Pipeline Trail, which can be used to shorten this hike, diverges to the right. Keep right where

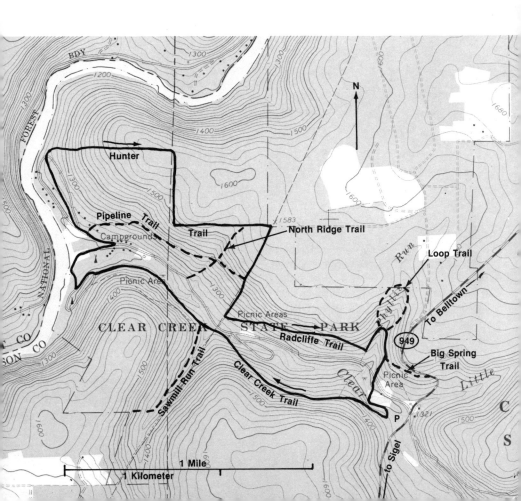

Clear Creek Trail

the road splits. You can avoid some of this road walking by using the jogging trail to your left—at some risk of being run over by a speeding jogger.

Bear right to the River Trail at 3.6 km (2.3 miles), cross the paved road, and shortly turn right on the Hunter Trail. You now begin the only real climb on this hike.

The Hunter Trail is marked both with the standard white diamond blazes and with large irregularly-shaped white blazes. The latter show that this trail separates the part of the park open to hunting on your left from the part closed to hunting on your right.

The top of the hill is reached at 4.3 km (2.7 miles), and shortly the trail turns right. It continues in this new direction until it reaches the edge of Clear Creek Valley. After starting to descend, it turns sharply left, regains the hilltop, and continues past a junction with the North Ridge Trail at 5.7 km (3.6 miles). Turn right on the pipeline and note the larch trees planted here to soften the visual impact of the swath.

A large boulder at 6.0 km (3.8 miles) provides a view across the valley. The swath is a good place to see deer. Soon the Pipeline Trail joins from the right, and you turn left on the Radcliffe Trail at 6.3 km (3.9 miles). The Radcliffe Trail proceeds through a plantation of white pine and Norway spruce. Where the trail meets some red pine, it jogs farther up the hillside.

At 7.4 km (4.6 miles) turn left on the Phyllis Run Trail in the midst of another spruce plantation. You get several good views of Phyllis Run as you pass an unsafe piped spring. Bypass the longer loop, cross Phyllis Run, and head back down the other side. Shortly the Big Spring Trail diverges left, and at 7.9 km (4.9 miles) you turn left on the paved park road. Keep right, and in only 50 meters you find a flight of steps leading down to several picnic shelters. Cut through the picnic area to the dam and use the footbridge to cross. A plaque says the dam was built by the Civilian Conservation Corps in 1934. Beyond the dam, turn left and pass between the beach and beach house to the gated access road. You are back at the beach house parking lot.

This hike uses only four of the 17 trails in Clear Creek State Park. There is plenty of additional hiking here and across PA 949 in Clear Creek State Forest with its Beartown Rocks Trail.

21

Slater Run

Distance: 8.7 km (5.5 miles)
Time: 3 hours
Rise: 200 meters (650 feet)
Highlights: Tanbark Trail; mountain streams
Maps: USGS 7½' Cobham, Youngsville; Hiker's Guide to
* Allegheny National Forest, map no. 12*

This hike uses the northernmost portion of the Tanbark Trail and an old railroad grade to take you on a delightful circuit hike in the Allegheny Front area. The tanbark referred to is that of the eastern hemlock, Tsuga canadensis. In the nineteenth century, tannic acid was extracted from hemlock bark and used to tan hides. It was cheaper to bring the hides to the bark than the bark to the hides, so Penn's Woods was filled with tanneries, large and small. The leather companies bought large tracts of hemlock to assure themselves a supply of bark. On occasion, hemlock was cut solely for its bark and the logs left to rot in the woods.

About the turn of the century, 65 of the 120 largest tanneries formed the United State Leather Company. U.S. Leather then formed Central Pennsylvania Lumber Company to cut its hemlock forests. But time was running out for the tanneries. Most of the hemlock were soon gone, and the tanneries began to close. Many of the towns they had spawned became ghost towns. Much of the leather was used for harnesses for horses, mules and oxen. With the coming of the internal combustion engine,

the harness market collapsed. Leather was also used for belts to run machines in factories, but the electric motor largely eliminated this application. Synthetic tannic acid was developed ending the need for natural supplies. So the Tanbark Trail reminds us of the rise and fall of the tanning industry in Penn's Woods.

The Allegheny Front Area is one of the four largest roadless areas in Allegheny National Forest. It is bordered by US 62 on the west and old PA 337 on the east. It includes most or all of the valleys of Slater and South Slater Runs, Boarding House Run, Clark Run, Hedgehog Run and Charley Run. Oil and gas drilling precludes Allegheny Front from designation as a wilderness area.

The trailhead is located on US 62, 8.9 miles south of the old PA 337 junction in Tidioute and 6.7 miles south of US 6. There is ample parking on the river side of the highway, both north and south of the Tanbark trailhead. Hiking boots are in order, owing to many wet areas and a steep scramble up the side of a road cut on US 62.

To start the hike, head south along

US 62. Keep to the left side, facing the heavy traffic. This part isn't much fun, so hurry along. You are looking for the old railroad grade up the hillside, but it can't be seen from the highway. Avoid a couple of old roads on private land. They aren't railroads. The public land is at the steepest part of the hillside. The old railroad grade is 0.9 km (0.6 mile) from the Tanbark trailhead, and your landmark is a small sign facing the other way which says 6/50. The sign is a state transportation department distance marker. Here you scramble up the steep bank above the sign. A few meters north, the railroad grade has been destroyed by the highway. A few meters south it is even higher above the road.

Once you gain the old railroad grade, turn right and climb higher still. A footway is discernible along the outside of the old railroad. Early logging railroads were innocent of surveying. They were usually narrow gauge and so poorly built that one can have great difficulty following them today. This railroad appears to be a late model. It is standard gauge, and the even gradient indicates good surveying.

The trail makes a cool dark tunnel under the large hemlock. At 1.2 km (0.8 mile) bear left at a fork in the railroad grade. You immediately cross under a pole line and can see a house to the right. The railroad continues through hemlock groves. You can hear Slater Run below, but you won't see it for some time although many blowdowns have been cleared with a chainsaw.

At 2.1 km (1.3 miles) keep left where a faint trail diverges to the right. The hillside becomes rockier with conglomerate and sandstone boulders, some of them quite large. Another trail converges from the right at 3.1 km (1.9 miles). Here a boulder has slid partway across the grade, evidence that these rocks do move on occasion.

Soon you come to a side stream with considerable flow, one of many wet places. Next you reach the edge of the mountain laurel belt. I suspect the laurel is associated with a certain layer of bedrock. At 3.9 km (2.4 miles) Slater Run is close at hand and a faint trail leads over to this appealing mountain stream. The railroad grade has become poorly defined. However, it doesn't make any wild turns, so continue ahead.

The mountain laurel closes in to define the trail. A bullet-riddled pipe sticking out of the ground at 4.3 km (2.7 miles) is the only sign of oil drilling on this hike. Cross Slater Run and continue to climb very gently, leaving the mountain laurel behind.

The signed junction with the blue-"eye"-blazed Tanbark Trail is reached at 5.0 km (3.1 miles). Turn left and cross Slater Run on a bridge. Then climb past a campsite at the top of the bank and continue climbing to the broad ridge top. At 6.1 km (3.8 miles) turn left on an old road.

After a bit, you notice that you are now descending slowly. Next you can see Boarding House Run to your right among some fair-sized hemlock. The Tanbark Trail is now definitely descending. After crossing a side stream, you bear right off the old road at 8.4 km (5.3 miles) and descend steeply among large black cherry and hemlock trees. As you cross the pole line swath, you get a good view of Boarding House Run. A few more steps and you are back at the highway.

This hike could be extended by following the Tanbark out to the Sandstone Springs picnic area on SR 3005 before taking it down Boarding House Run.

22

Mill Creek Game Lands

In-and-out distance: 9.8 km (5.8 miles)
Time: 3 hours
Rise: 30 meters (100 feet)
Highlight: Baker Trail
Maps: USGS 7½' Corsica; Baker Trail Guide Book map #14;
  Sportsmen's Recreation Map—State Game Lands 74

One of the nicest sections of the Baker Trail runs south of Cook Forest, crossing State Game Lands No. 74 along Mill Creek. (This is a different Mill Creek than the one in Allegheny National Forest.)

In the early nineteenth century, when water was the only dependable source

Deer Tracks

of power, nearly every stream had one or more grist mills or sawmills. Eventually, coal replaced water as a source of energy. Much of the coal in western Pennsylvania is a high-sulfur variety. Air and water work together to convert this sulfur into sulfuric acid, causing acid mine drainage from old mines which is quite harmful to nearby waterways. Currently the only way to prevent this acid mine drainage is to strip mine the coal seam in question, which destroys the old mine tunnels. Since many old mines are very shallow, much acid mine drainage could be eliminated, provided that strip mining is done in accordance with Pennsylvania law.

While the lower part of Mill Creek, which you cross on the way to the trailhead, shows evidence of acid mine drainage, the upper part of Mill Creek in Game Lands 74 appears to be free of it. There is even some life in the stream.

Game Lands 74 is located north of I-80 and east of Clarion. The trailhead is a bit complicated to reach, so pay careful attention. From exit 11 on I-80, take US 322 west for about 4 miles to Strattanville. Turn right on Perry Street and follow it northeast for 6.7 miles to the crossroads of Fisher, crossing Mill Creek and the game lands along the way. Turn right at the church and go south for 1.2 miles. Here you bear left and fol-

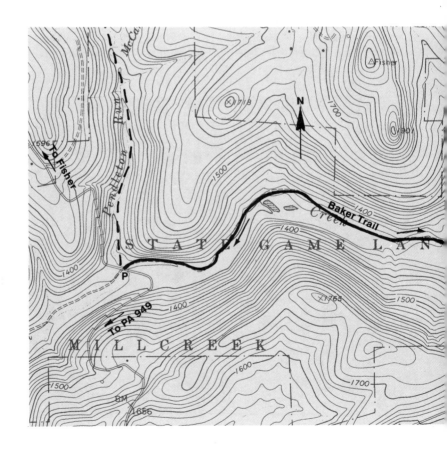

low the road down into Mill Creek Valley for 1.4 miles to a parking area, just before a bridge over the creek. You may park on either side of the road, but there is more shade on the left. Several ways to shortcut this approach to the trailhead can be found with the help of the game commission map and dry roads. You could also arrange a car shuttle.

Ordinary walking shoes should be fine for this hike. If you want to wear your hiking boots, they will help you cross Pendleton and Updike Runs.

To start the hike, step over or around the gate on the emergency road near the creek. Make sure you are headed upstream on Mill Creek, not Pendleton Run, which you must cross immediately on stepping stones. Pendleton Run supports a growth of hemlock and rhododendron.

Just beyond, you join the yellow-blazed Baker Trail and continue upstream along Mill Creek on the game commission management road. Trees along this trail are black cherry, white oak, red maple, occasional white pine, and many hemlock, large and small. Don't be alarmed if you see blazes at right angles to the trail. They do not indicate a turn but are only a curious variation of blazing on the Baker Trail. Occasionally, unmarked trails lead off to

the creek.

At 2.2 km (1.4 miles) the creek comes back to your side of the valley, and soon you reach a large game food plot. There is also some aspen around the borders of this meadow but no evidence of beaver. The game commission road ends here at the food plot, but continue across the plot in a straight line. At the far side, you cross Updike Run and pick up the trail again on an old woods road.

The trail jogs left at 3.2 km (2.0 miles) and climbs a bank. Here you enter a dark enchanted forest of hemlock. Continue through the hemlock to 4.7 km (2.9 miles) where you meet a road. This road marks the turn-around point. The Baker Trail bears right on this road and leaves the game lands. At the next road junction it continues on private land north of Mill Creek. Retrace your steps to your car.

Also in Game Lands 74 you could follow the Baker Trail up Pendleton Run or follow the management road downstream from the parking area. At one time the North Country Trail was to follow Baker to this point and then head downstream along Mill Run. It appears now that it will follow the Clarion River on lands recently acquired by the Western Pennsylvania Conservancy.

23

Cook Forest State Park

Distance: 10.2 km (6.3 miles)
Time: 4 hours
Rise: 370 meters (1,220 feet)
Highlights: Virgin timber; lookout tower
Maps: USGS 7½' Cooksburg; state park map; Baker Trail
  maps

Logging started early in what is now Cook Forest State Park. John Cook began cutting along Toms Run in 1828. Rafts made of squared white pine logs were floated to Pittsburgh. This business was continued by Cook's son, Anthony, and then in turn by the grandchildren. A small patch of timber, only a short distance from the sawmill on Toms Run, had been left standing with the intention that it be cut just before the sawmill was dismantled. In the 1920s, the Cook Forest Association raised $200,000, and with $450,000 from the state, used it to purchase Cook Forest State Park. Thus one of the largest stands of virgin white pine was saved from the axe. At other locations in the park virgin hemlock is found. But what man has saved, nature may still ravage. Violent wind storms, one in 1956 and another in 1976, devastated different parts of the forest, felling windrows of trees. The park has also been damaged by floods. In June 1981, one flood washed out several footbridges across Toms Run, severing the Baker and other trails. This hike visits several areas of virgin timber, Cook Forest fire tower and a lookout over the Clarion River, using parts of the Baker Trail not destroyed in the storms of 1976 and 1981.

Cook Forest State Park is on PA 36, about 15 miles north of exit 13 on I-80 at Brookville. This hike starts from the Log Cabin Inn Visitor Center on the Vowinckel Road, 1 mile north of the junction with PA 36 in Cooksburg. There is abundant parking space and restrooms are available at the adjacent picnic area. There are wet areas along this hike but the footway is generally good, so you should be able to do the hike with ordinary walking shoes.

To start the hike, turn left on the paved road facing traffic and cross the stone bridge over Toms Run. Pass the Liggett-Baker Trail (see Hike 31) and continue to shelter no. 1 where you cross the road and head up the Ridge Trail. The climb passes among large hemlock and you reach the top of the hill at 900 meters. At the end of the Ridge Trail in the campground, turn left on the paved road and follow it out to PA 36 at 1.6 km (1.0 mile).

Cross the highway and bear right on the exit from the one way road to the

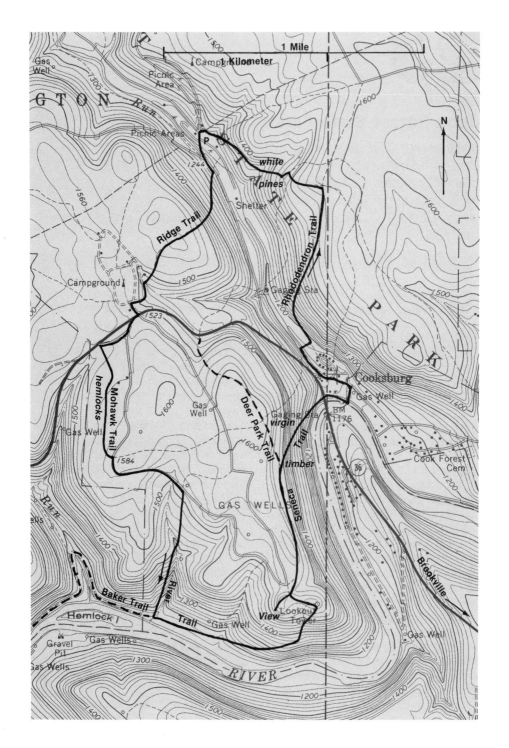

lookout tower. Where the exit road splits, keep right on the part that heads you back to the highway. At the point where you return to PA 36, find the Mohawk Trail and turn left. Immediately you are in a beautiful stand of virgin hemlock interspersed with a few white pines and giant beech. At 2.9 km (1.8 miles) turn right on the Tower Road. At the top of a rise look carefully for the River Trail crossing and turn right on this trail at 3.5 km (2.2 miles). The River Trail descends to the Clarion and about halfway down there is a confusing stretch where the trail splits into several paths. The trail you want crosses the bottom of the draw and continues down the far side. There are several large stands of rhododendron along this part of the River Trail as well as a patch of mountain laurel.

At the bottom of the hill the Baker Trail comes in from the right past a natural gas well. The Baker Trail is not blazed through the park but is marked with signs at trail junctions and road crossings. Take a good look at the Clarion, down which you can see Hemlock Island, and then turn left (upstream), still on the River Trail. There is more rhododendron along the river.

At 4.8 km (3.0 miles) you cross a meadow and then a side stream. Next, the trail draws away from the river and climbs back up the hill. The climb continues to the base of Cook Forest lookout tower. The best views from the top are north up Toms Run and east up the Clarion.

Back on the ground, follow the heavily used trail to the Seneca Trail junction and turn left to Seneca Point. Seneca Point is a natural vista down the Clarion River. Then backtrack on the Seneca Trail and continue past the restrooms and parking area along the edge of the hill. At 6.8 km (4.2 miles) the Deer Park Trail diverges to the left and you start

down the side of the hill through another stand of virgin hemlock and white pine. Soon you enter the area damaged by the tornado of 11 July 1976. The trail has been reestablished so it is still easy to follow, and there is a view of the Clarion below. Soon you reenter the woods—the trail is dug into the steep hillside—and continue to the bottom of the slope.

At 7.6 km (4.7 miles) you cross PA 36 with care and continue on the River Road, passing the park office. Turn left on the paved road and circle around an enclave of private land, passing the children's fishing pond and the Indian Cabins. Turn right on the Birch and Rhododendron Trail just before you reach PA 36. Turn right at 8.2 km (5.1 miles) and cross the swing bridge over Toms Run. At the far side turn right and then left to pick up the Rhododendron Trail, which has already started its climb up the hill. Turn left on the Rhododendron Trail and climb gently on its fine old grade. At 9.1 km (5.7 miles) turn left on the Joyce Kilmer Trail and then shortly turn left again at a junction with the Indian Trail. At the next junction continue ahead on the Longfellow and Baker Trail which you follow down the hill.

This is the heart of the forest cathedral. The 60 meter white pine you find here are truly awesome. An ordinary white pine would top off where the first branches on these monarchs begin. Were all Penns Woods like this from the lake to the sea only 200 years ago? Considering all the demands on forests today—not only timber and pulp but firewood, biomass and even a new resource base for the chemical industry—can any forest on this planet ever be left long enough to grow trees like these again?

Continue down the Longfellow Trail or

Clarion River

wander up and down the lettered side trails (see park map) as the spirit moves you. At 10.1 km (6.3 miles) on the Longfellow Trail pass the memorial fountain and emerge at the Log Cabin Inn Visitor Center. Stop in to see the exhibits on display before returning to your car.

This hike has used only ten of the 43 kilometers (27 miles) of hiking trails in Cook Forest State Park, so there are many additional hiking opportunities. The CCC Trail, just north of the visitor center, is one. See also Hike 31, which leads you into the more remote regions along Browns Run.

Hemlock Run

Distance: 11.0 km (6.8 miles)
Time: 4 hours
Rise: 90 meters (300 feet)
Highlight: North Country Trail; mountain stream
Maps: USGS 7½′ Cornplanter Bridge, Westline; Allegheny
National Forest Hiking Guide, maps 2 and 3

The National Trails System Act of 1968 designated the Pacific Crest Trail and the Appalachian Trail as National Scenic Trails. The act named fourteen other trails for study and possible addition to the system. One of these was the North Country Trail, from Crown Point in New York to the Missouri River in North Dakota. If completed, the North Country Trail will extend about 5,100 kilometers (3,200 miles), the longest in the world. In l980, Congress designated the North Country Trail as a National Scenic Trail, but said it must be built by volunteers. Meanwhile, a section of the North Country Trail, 160 kilometers (100 miles) long, had already been built across Allegheny National Forest, from the New York state line to Pennsylvania State Game Land 24, where it joins the Baker Trail. Much of the North Country Trail in Allegheny National Forest was built by the Allegheny Outdoor Club. The Baker Trail was built by the Pittsburgh Council of the American Youth Hostels.

This hike follows an exceptionally appealing section of the North Country Trail along Hemlock Run, between PA 59 and PA 321 at Chappel Fork. It is or-

ganized as a car shuttle hike, and it is almost entirely downhill. The car shuttle is simple. Leave one car at the end of the hike on PA 321. Caution! The North Country Trail crosses PA 321 at two different places. The crossing you want is the more northern one. It is 4.5 miles south of the junction with PA 59 at Bradford Ranger Station. The crossing is signed, and there is parking for several cars on the west side of the road. Drive your other car north 4.5 miles and turn left on PA 59 for 2.3 miles. The North Country Trail crossing of PA 59 is also signed, and there is parking for a few cars on Forest Road 265. Additional parking is available south of PA 59. The many stream crossing make this a low-water hike, and you should wear hiking boots.

To start the hike, continue along Forest Road 265. There are no blazes along this section. At 0.2 km (0.1 mile) the forest road is gated off, and you turn right on an old road. There is no sign at this turn, but here you pick up the white "eye" blazes. (Beware, Allegheny National Forest is considering a change to plastic blazes nailed to trees.)

At 0.6 km (0.4 mile) you bear right off the old road, but at 0.8 km (0.5 mile) you bear right again on what appears to be the same road. A structure, apparently abandoned, is visible through the trees to the left. A variation of the "eye" blaze is used along this section to mark turns. The small rectangle is placed on the side of the large rectangle to indicate the direction of the turn. This is effective, but it does take a large tree to carry the blaze.

At 1.0 km (0.6 mile) continue straight ahead where another road diverges to the left, and soon you cross a small meadow. Jog left across Forest Road 517 at 2.1 km (1.3 miles), passing a large serviceberry. The small stream to your left is Hemlock Run, and you will follow it as it cuts its way down to Chappel Bay. Smaller streams enter from each side, and Hemlock Run grows with each addition. Hemlock Run makes a deeper cut into the plateau where you come to some large sandstone and conglomerate boulders, on their slow slide into the stream.

At 3.4 km (2.1 miles) you cross the corner of a clearing past House Rock. When viewed through the trees the slanting sides of House Rock look like the roof of a cabin. The first crossing of Hemlock Run is at 3.7 km (2.3 miles) but the next isn't until 4.3 km (2.7 miles). Three more come in rapid succession. At the last of these note the large hemlock.

Farther along you pick up an old railroad grade, and the valley begins to widen out. At 5.9 km (3.7 miles) there are two more crossings of Hemlock Run, and at 6.8 km (4.3 miles) there are another two crossings. Occasionally, the trail climbs the bank to avoid a crossing. The railroad must have transported logs to the Central Pennsylvania Lumber Company mill at Kinzua. This town is now submerged beneath Allegheny Reservoir.

Turn left at 7.6 km (4.6 miles). Ahead,

Mountain ash

you can see the waters of Chappel Bay. The railroad continues beneath them, on its way to the sunken city of Kinzua. As you continue along the hillside, you soon pick up an old road. At 8.6 km (5.4 miles) you jog right across a pipeline swath. Below you, Chappel Fork is already a free flowing stream again. Turn left on another Central Pennsylvania Lumber railroad grade and follow it into a meadow studded with old apple trees along Chappel Run. At one point, the trail goes right to the edge of the run, and this may have been a crossing site. But there has been a relocation, and you bear left into the woods again.

At 9.3 km (5.8 miles) you cross Briggs Run, and then turn left for a short climb to another pipeline swath. Turn right on this swath and follow it through a small clearing and then into another meadow with more old apple trees. Turn right off the pipeline and follow an old road to a meadow where you cross under a wooden-poled power line at 10.7 km (6.7 miles). Soon you come to the footbridge over Chappel Fork. A dirt road takes you directly to the trailhead parking on PA 321.

You can hike farther along the North Country Trail. The trail continues south across PA 321 and climbs over the hill to cross PA 321 again near Red Bridge camping area, a distance of about ten kilometers (6.2 miles). It continues north of PA 59 to Sugar Run, about eight more kilometers (5 miles). The Rimrock-Morrison loop trail is about two miles west on PA 59 (Hike 26).

25

Chapman State Park

Distance: 9.5 km (5.9 miles)
Time: 3½ hours
Rise: 287 meters (940 feet)
Highlight: A nice walk in the woods
Maps: USGS 7½' Cherry Grove, Warren; state park map

Chapman State Park is a pleasant little park, only 324 hectares (800 acres) on the West Branch of Tionesta Creek near Warren. It is bordered by Allegheny National Forest, State Game Land 29, and a couple of tracts of private land. The park's trails are unusually well developed but have to be continuously relocated and rebuilt as required by timber sales. For the moment the threat of oil and gas well drilling seems to have lifted but the state does not own the oil, gas or mineral rights under Chapman Park. Even the federal government owns only one to two percent of these rights in the giant Allegheny National Forest. Any new surge in oil and gas prices would bring the drillers bulldozing their way into the park.

Chapman Park is at the end of a paved road leading west out of Clarendon on US 6 between Warren and Sheffield. From the turn at the traffic light in Clarendon, it is 5.0 miles to the picnic area just below the dam where this hike begins. Ordinary walking shoes should suffice but there are plenty of wet spots. At the time this hike was redone the Penny Run Trail was closed because of the collapse of a bridge for cross-country skiers. Hikers can easily cross this

ravine so the Penny Run Trail is retained in this hike.

Cross the park road to the Penny Run Trail and squeeze around the gate. The trail is marked with occasional white Ts painted on the trees. Farther along, some of the blue plastic diamonds have survived. This trail was rebuilt by the Youth Conservation Corps in 1980 and mostly uses old roads. It climbs first through open woods to 0.6 km (0.4 mile) where it swings left to avoid some wet spots. It then returns to the old road and continues to 1.0 km (0.6 mile) where the bridge has collapsed. Just beyond, it reaches a corner of Allegheny National Forest. Here you turn right and follow another old road across half a dozen bridges to 1.4 km (0.9 mile) where you turn right and descend along yet another old road. At 1.7 km (1.1 miles) you cross a bridge over Penny Run. Bear right at 2.2 km (1.4 miles) to reach the paved park road.

Turn left along the park road and follow it to 2.7 km (1.7 miles) where you pass a vehicle gate and head up the Lumber Trail. Keep right where a road goes uphill to the reservoir but turn right at 3.0 km (1.9 miles) on the Nature Trail which is again marked with white Ts

painted on trees. The sign faces and points in the wrong direction at this junction. Follow the Nature Trail downhill through a hemlock grove. At the bottom, cross a stream and then turn upstream to circle the upper campground loop.

At 3.8 km (2.4 miles) you reach a junction of Nature Trail loops. Turn left here and cross a bridge. There are numbered posts along this part of the Nature Trail. Avoid an unmarked trail to the right at 4.2 km (2.6 miles) but turn left on the Game Lands Trail at 4.3 km

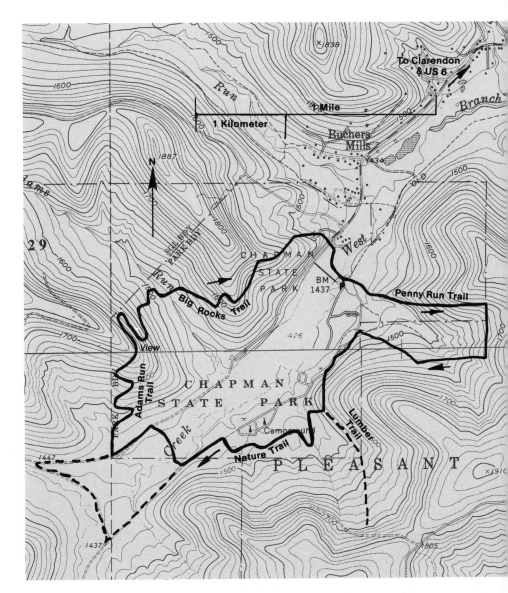

Swing bridge over West Branch of Tionesta Creek

(2.7 miles). This trail is the bed of the old Tionesta Valley Railroad.

Turn right at 4.5 km (2.8 miles) on the Lowlands Trail and cross the swing bridge over the West Branch of Tionesta Creek. At 4.9 km (3.0 miles) turn left on the Adams Run Trail and follow it to the boundary of State Game Land No. 29. Here you turn right and switchback up the hill. This trail is marked by red discs with white arrows on them. At the top of the hill this trail picks up a logging road. Follow this to a junction at 6.6 km (4.1 miles). Turn left here past a bench. By standing on this bench you can get a glimpse across the lake. This seems to be the overlook referred to on the park map. The Adams Run Trail switchbacks down the hillside to a junction with the Big Rocks Trail at 7.5 km (4.7 miles).

Turn left on the Big Rocks Trail, cross a bridge over Adams Run and climb along this cross country ski trail that was cleared by Keystone Trails Association Trail Care Team in July 1987. When I rehiked this trail in 1989 it was unmarked but still obvious. Follow the obvious logging grade over the hill. The

Big Rocks Trail has been relocated away from all the big rocks. Keep left at a junction of logging grades at 8.2 km (5.1 miles) and bear right at another junction at 8.6 km (5.3 miles). Just a bit farther down the slope you pass through an old apple orchard. The apple trees give way to an evergreen plantation. Keep left at a trail junction and continue along the edge of a pit. Then bear right into some evergreens and turn right along the edge of the meadow beyond. At the bottom of the meadow you reach a junction of hard roads across from the park office. Take the one ahead for the parking lot below the dam where you left your car.

This hike could be extended by following the Game Lands Trail onto SGL 29 to its junction with the management road. Turn right on the management road, follow it across the West Branch of Tionesta Creek and turn on the Adams Run Trail just after reaching the park boundary. Otherwise, this hike has used almost all the trails in Chapman State Park.

26

Morrison Trail

Distance: 15.3 km (9.5 miles)
Time: 5¼ hours
Rise: 330 meters (1,080 feet)
Highlights: Mountain stream and waterfalls
Map: USGS 7½' Cornplanter Bridge

Morrison Trail is a circuit trail in Allegheny National Forest between PA 59 and the Kinzua arm of Allegheny Reservoir. It was laid out and cleared by the Allegheny Outdoor Club. Originally blazed as an 18.5 kilometer (11.5 miles) loop with a cutoff, the eastern part of the loop has now been re-opened after some logging. By using the Morrison campground, roughly halfway around, this hike could be turned into a two-day backpack. But leaving a car on PA 59 overnight is not advisable. The trailhead is located on the south side of the highway, 4.3 miles west of PA 321 and the Bradford ranger station and 0.8 mile east of the road to Rimrock Overlook. Because of the many wet spots and the rocky trail, hiking boots are in order.

Start your hike by following the blue "eye" blazes south away from the highway. (Beware, Allegheny National Forest may change to plastic markers nailed to trees.) The trail passes through open woods to the loop junction at 0.8 km (0.5 mile). Turn right and follow the trail across a stream to the junction with the connector trail on which you will return. Continue ahead. The trail here is cut through thickets of mountain laurel. In

most years, the laurel blooms in the last week of June. The best displays are usually those patches exposed to direct sunlight. Serviceberries, some of them good-sized trees, are also found along this section.

Next you pass by a fenced clearing to the right. In 1988 the trees here were defoliated by gypsy moths. It usually takes several years of defoliation to kill oaks but the drought of 1988 finished these off in one year. The U.S. Forest Service salvaged the dead trees and planted oak seedlings to replace them. The fence is to keep the deer out so the seedlings will have a chance to grow. Each seedling is marked with a white plastic post. Solar ultraviolet will destroy these posts in six or seven years.

At 2.4 km (1.5 miles) turn left on an old logging road. This begins a particularly pleasant section of the hike. A clearing to the right of the trail is passed at 2.9 km (1.8 miles), and shortly you bear left. At 3.7 km (2.3 miles) you turn left at a fork in the old logging road, and soon you turn right onto the trail.

Along this section, look for the ghostly Indian pipe flower. The Indian pipe is a saprophyte. It lives on dead and decaying organic material, like a fungus. Along the stems you can see tiny vestigial leaves—totally devoid of chlorophyll.

At 4.7 km (2.9 miles) you start to descend into Campbell Run. Soon you cross a side stream and then continue among large conglomerate boulders. Conglomerate looks like concrete, but it is really a very coarse sandstone in which pebble-sized chunks of still older rocks have been cemented together.

A bit farther down the ravine the trail picks up an old road and follows it, except for a detour around a wet place. At 5.7 km (3.6 miles) turn left off the old road and start to cut across the steep slope that drops into the reservoir below. Here, the trail passes among some large hemlock. You can hear power boats on the reservoir even though you can't see them. At 6.1 km (3.8 miles) you can see the reservoir through the trees as you cross an old log skid. Log skids were troughs, lubricated with oil or ice, used to slide logs downhill.

Bear left on another old road on which you can climb far up the slope. Along the way you pass a white pine. Farther up, you cross a couple of streams and then bear right off the old road onto the trail, which passes among more large boulders.

At 7.0 km (4.4 miles) you cross a stream at the edge of a meadow and then continue on a more recent logging road. Soon you come to a view of the reservoir from the top of a large con-

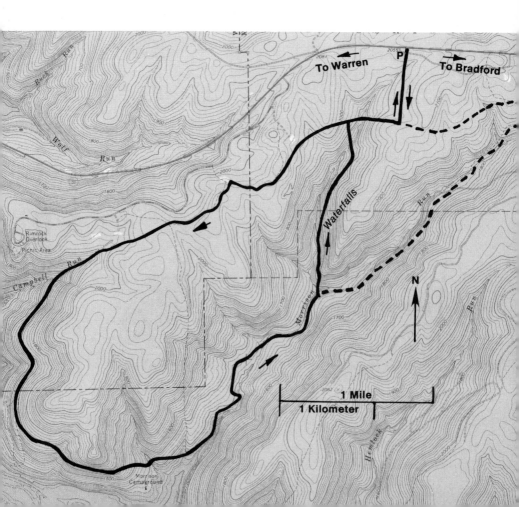

Morrison Run

glomerate boulder; the view could be much improved if a single black birch was removed.

At 7.5 km (4.7 miles) bear left off the logging road past some dogwood and continue across the slope on rough trail. Along this stretch you pass a pair of white pines. You cross another old log skid at 8.2 km (5.1 miles) and again you can see the water below through the trees. At 8.9 km (5.5 miles) you reach the corner of a meadow with a view of the reservoir. As you continue along the edge of the meadow you pass old apple trees and highbush blueberry. The trail then enters the meadow, and you see crab apple and hawthorn growing here, as well as some spruce that have been planted.

At 9.2 km (5.8 miles) you cross a trail that leads to Morrison campground. Your trail now begins to swing upstream along Morrison Run, crossing a few side streams, and then picks up an old road. A critical turn is reached at 10.1 km (6.3 miles) where you turn sharply right off the old road and drop down to Morrison Run. At the run, you move upstream, staying on the west side. (Camping is also permitted a short way up Morrison Run.) You continue upstream, some-times following what appears to be an old railroad grade to 12.2 km (7.6 miles), where you come to the Forks of the Morrison, in a small meadow. To avoid the eastern part of the loop and take the cutoff, you must turn up the left fork here. Almost immediately, you cross the left fork, and soon you step across it again. Climbing along the left fork is steeper than the main stream.

Soon you notice small waterfalls in the stream below, and then you come to a mini-glen. The Morrison has saved the best for the last. Giant boulders have slid into the stream here, forming water-falls. Soon you cross the left fork again and then climb steeply through some more large boulders to an old road at 13.2 km (8.3 miles). Turn left and con-tinue to 13.7 km (8.5 miles), where you turn left and climb to a junction with the loop trail at 14.1 km (8.8 miles). Turn right on the loop trail and then left on the access trail to reach PA 59 and the trailhead.

The best bet for further hiking in this part of the woods is the North Country Trail that crosses PA 59 two miles to the east (Hike 24). Also, you could extend your hike by taking the eastern part of the loop rather than the cutoff.

27

Tracy Ridge Trail

Distance: 16.7 km (10.3 miles)
Time: 5½ hours
Rise: 360 meters (1,200 feet)
Highlight: North Country Trail
Maps: USGS 7½' Cornplanter Run, Stickney; Allegheny
National Forest Hiking Guide, map 1

Another large roadless area in Allegheny National Forest is Tracy Ridge in the northern part of the forest, just south of the New York border. The area is bounded by PA 321 on the east, Willow Bay Recreational Area on the north, Allegheny Reservoir on the west and Sugar Bay on the south. Tracy Ridge has been granted National Recreation Area status.

This hike is a daylong circuit, following parts of the Johnnycake and North Country trails as well as Tracy Ridge. It could probably be done with good walking shoes, at least during the drier times of the year. The hike could be turned into a two day backpack by using the Handsome Lake campground, south of Johnnycake Run on the North Country Trail. But it is not advisable to leave cars overnight at the trailhead on PA 321. There is additional parking in the Tracy Ridge Campground.

The Tracy Ridge Trail parking lot is on the west side of PA 321, 2.6 miles south of the junction with PA 346, 0.4 mile north of the entrance to Tracy Ridge campground, and 11.0 miles north of the junction with PA 59.

Step over the log restricting motor access to an old fire road and start your hike on the Tracy Ridge Trail. At 0.3 km (0.2 mile) turn left on the trail that's blue-blazed. The so-called "eye" blazes, popular in Allegheny National Forest, are used here. These blazes consist of a small horizontal rectangle above a larger vertical rectangle. When done correctly on reasonably smooth bark, they resemble the letter "i." They do avoid confusion with trees marked for sale but create problems at turns and intersections. (Beware, Allegheny National Forest may change to plastic markers nailed to trees.) There used to be trail signs at all of these points, but half or more of them were missing at the time of my trip.

At 0.8 km (0.5 mile) bear right where the gray-blazed Land of Many Uses Interpretive trail goes left toward Tracy Ridge campground. Partway past some big rocks at 1.2 km (0.8 mile) the trail turns sharply left and proceeds through a narrow passage. The campground is visible through the trees. Beyond the rocks, you bear right and continue to an old jeep road at 1.6 km (1.0 mile) where you jog right. You reach the johnnycake Trail junction at 2.2 km (1.4 miles). You

RESERVOIR

NORMAL POOL ELEV 1328

Tracy

Deer Lick

Run

Tracy Run

Run

North Country Trail

TRACY RUN

Tracy Ridge Trail

TRAIL

Whisky Run

Run

Run

×2021

2100

1900

1800

2052

2000

1900

JOHNNYCAKE

BM 1674

NATIONAL

FOREST

CO

Johnnycake

Run

To Handsome
Lake Campground

2011 ×

will return on the Johnnycake Trail to this point. Caution, this junction is signed only for the interpretive trail, which turns left on the Johnnycake Trail. But now turn right and continue on Tracy Ridge Trail. Tracy Ridge is broad and flat, so you don't begin to see its edge until you are well along. As the ridge narrows, you swing over the left side to start down to Allegheny Reservoir. This is a new trail, built to avoid a steep drop down the ridge line itself. Soon you swing back to the ridge line and continue to descend.

At 6.7 km (4.2 miles)—the bottom of the hill—you reach a junction with the white-blazed North Country Trail. To your right, the North Country Trail leads to Allegany State Park in New York. (Yes, there is a different spelling on the other side of the state line.) The reservoir can be seen through the trees. The North Country Trail cuts across the steep hillside that drops into the reservoir. Keep an eye out for highbush blueberry. They probably never bear much under the trees, but you might find a few berries in July.

Along the hillside you cross a number of streams of various sizes. Whisky Run is the largest of these, and you cross it at 9.4 km (5.9 miles). At 10.1 km (6.3 miles) you pass through an open grove of white pine. The North Country Trail now swings eastward in order to round Johnnycake Run inlet on the reservoir. Johnnycake Trail and Run are reached at 10.6 km (6.6 miles). The North Country Trail crosses the run and continues to Handsome Lake campground and, eventually, to North Dakota. A vista over the reservoir has been cut just south of Johnnycake Bay. Turn left and follow the blue-blazed Johnnycake Trail upstream.

At 11.4 km (7.1 miles) note evidence of an old corduroy road at a side stream crossing. Johnnycake Run itself is crossed at 11.7 km (7.3 miles) and again at 12.1 km (7.6 miles). At 14.2 km (8.9 miles) you pass a junction with the Interpretive Trail on your right, and at the top of the hill you bear right on the Tracy Ridge Trail. From here you retrace your steps to your car.

This hike could be extended by following the North Country Trail either to the north or south. The only other hike appears to be the 4 km (2.5 miles) Interpretive Trail around the campground. A new parking lot for trail users has been built in the Tracy Ridge Campground.

Brush Hollow Trail

Distance: 10.4 km (6.4 miles)
Time: 3¾ hours
Rise: 160 meters (520 feet)
Highlights: Mountain streams, view
Maps: USGS 7½' James City; forestry map

Brush Hollow Trail is a set of three loop trails just west of Big Mill Creek in the Ridgway District of Allegheny National Forest. Primarily intended for cross-country skiing, the trail is also open to hikers year-round. This hike is a tour around the outside of this trail system.

Trails such as this one are quite a contrast to the old days of cross-country skiing. There were no plowed parking lots then. When you reached the trailhead, you piled out of the car and shoveled a spot to park. Then you put on your wooden skis—either heavy, unbreakable surplus from the 10th Mountain Division with cable bindings, or light and fragile skis with three-pin bindings. If you broke the tip of a wooden ski some distance from the trailhead, you could have real difficulty getting back. You had to carry a spare ski tip in your pack for emergency repairs.

Since nobody else knew about this trail, your group would have to break trail all day. When the person in the front of the line became exhausted, he or she would pull off to the side and let the next in line take over, dropping in again at the rear. Today's fiberglass skis are all but unbreakable, and usually you find the trail already tracked.

Beware! The Brush Hollow Trail System is open to mountain bikes—which quiet and fast. On occasion they run into hikers, with painful or even fatal results.

The trailhead is on PA 948, 10.7 miles northwest of its junction with US 219 in Ridgway and about 18 miles southeast of Sheffield. There is a sign on the highway. You'll find ample parking and an outhouse but no water at the parking lot. Despite some wet spots, walking shoes should be adequate for this hike. The loop trails permit you to shorten this hike. All the trails are marked with blue plastic diamonds nailed to trees, most with white arrows on them. The vertical rise is distributed along the hike.

To start your hike, head down the gated old road and then bear left on an old railroad grade above Mill Creek. Soon you pass a trail to the right that connects with the western part of Mill Creek Trail. There are repeated views of Mill Creek and its surrounding hemlocks.

Next, you reach a major trail junction at 0.8 km. Both ends of the Challenger Loop come in from the left. This is Brush Hollow itself. Note the bridge over the run. There are no steps, up or down, so you can ski right across it. All the bridges on the Brush Hollow Trail have been built to this standard. Note springs along the hillside.

Continue up Mill Creek. This valley was first logged by the firm of Hyde and Thayer, which had a sawmill downstream near the Clarion River. Hyde and Thayer used a series of three splash dams to float its logs down Mill Creek.

At the next junction cross Ellithorpe Run and continue upstream. Beech, yellow birch, and hemlock grow along the creek. In winter look for tracks of deer, wild turkey, and squirrel in the snow. Deer tracks show their cloven hooves. Turkey tracks look like those of a fossil dinosaur. Squirrel tracks are smaller and start or end near the base of a tree.

Next, the trail tunnels through a spruce plantation, swings left, and starts to climb the hill above Cherry Run, leaving the railroad grade behind. Logging railroads along Big Mill Creek were first built by Henry, Bayard and Company about 1897. After the timber was all cut, the track was pulled up. It was relaid in 1905 by the New York and Pennsylvania Company for its papermill in Johnsonburg. The New York and Pennsylvania cut the small hemlocks and hardwoods for pulp. It was the only paper company in Pennsylvania to use a logging railroad. See Thomas T. Tabor in *Tanbark, Alcohol, and Lumber.*

At 2.6 km turn left on a spur trail that leads to a leaves-off view down Big Mill Creek. This is a view for skiers; in summer you won't see a thing. (A clearing may be cut to make this view visible year-round, however.)

Return to the main trail and continue up the gentle grade to the broad ridgetop. Here you will find sugar maples and black cherry. Black cherry is now even more expensive than walnut for furniture. It is not appreciated much within the

Winter hiking

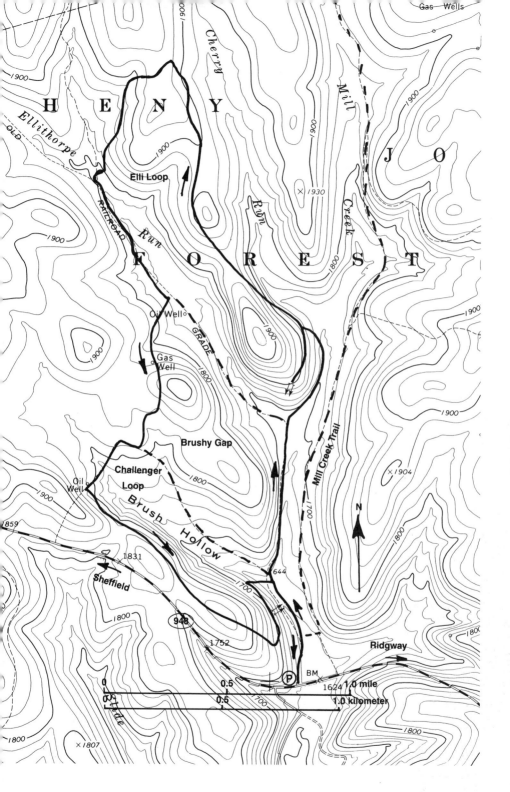

state, but as soon as you cross the border furniture salesmen whisper, "I can get it for you in Pennsylvania in black cherry—for only $1700 more."

The trail continues to follow an old grade along the top of the ridge, crossing and then recrossing a natural-gas pipeline. Oil production has ceased in the Big Mill Creek Valley, but natural-gas production continues.

Next, descend to Ellithorpe Run and cross on a bridge. Then turn downstream on a logging railroad grade. This was the longest spur of the railroad on Big Mill Creek, and Ellithorpe Valley was the last to be cut. By 1925 all cutting in Elk County was over.

Pass through a small stand of red pine and turn right to another grade. At 6.0 km, just after crossing a stream in a culvert, turn right on the Brushy Gap Loop and climb to a gas well at the top clearing, then descend gently to a junction with the Challenger Loop. Turn right and then left, crossing the run and passing an old oil well site. Bear left on a grade that slabs the north side of the ridge between Brush Hollow and PA 948. Finally, the trail emerges on the ridgetop.

Pass a grove of plastic tubes. These are used to protect seedlings from being eaten by deer. The interior of each tube retains a lot of moisture, and seedlings are said to grow twice as fast as they would in the open. When the tree emerges from the top of the tube, it should be too tough to be eaten. The tubes are then destroyed by solar ultraviolet radiation. Sugar maples appear to be planted in these tubes.

As you approach the end of the ridge there is a leaves-off view up Big Mill Creek. The trail then switchbacks to the left; this is the most difficult part of the trail system for cross-country skiers. Pass a year-round view up Big Mill Creek. Next, switchback to the right and reach the major trail junction at the end of Brush Hollow. Turn right on the railroad grade and retrace your steps to the parking lot.

Many additional hiking opportunities are found in this corner of Allegheny National Forest. First is the western part of the Mill Creek Loop Trail. The eastern part of this trail has been closed, so it can no longer be done as a circuit hike. Most of the trees along the eastern part died, letting full sunlight reach the forest floor. Seedlings, brush, and briers sprang up. Keeping the trail open would be a major undertaking in these times of shrinking budgets. The western part of the loop is still open. You passed the southern end of it on this hike. It can be hiked either on in-and-out basis or as a car shuttle from Twin Lakes Recreation Area.

The Buzzard Swamp Trail System near Marienville provides over 15 km of hiking and cross-country ski trails. Trailheads are on Forest Roads 157 and 130; there are four or more intersecting loops. Buzzard Swamp provides some the best wildlife viewing in Allegheny National Forest. With binoculars you may see bear, deer, beaver, coyote, snapping turtles, turkey, osprey, and bald eagles. In the spring migration you might see over 20 species of waterfowl.

The Twin Lakes Trail is a destination trail running 24 km from Twin Lakes Recreation Area to the North Country National Scenic Trail in Tionesta Scenic Area. See Hike 30.

Highway T 397 west of Ridgway provides two additional opportunities for hiking. The 18 km of the Laurel Mill X-C Ski and Hiking Area are 3 miles west, and the 5 km of the Little Drummer Historical Interpretive Trail are 8 miles west. Little Drummer refers to the drumming of grouse, for which the trail is named. One part of this trail follows the grade of the Tionesta Valley Railroad.

Hickory Creek Trail

Distance: 18.7 km (11.6 miles)
Time: 7 hours
Rise: 315 meters (1,030 feet)
Highlights: Pennsylvania's only congressionally designated
*   wilderness area, old logging camp*
Maps: USGS 7½' Cobham; U.S. Forest Service map

Hickory Creek Trail is located within a large roadless area in Allegheny National Forest. The trail is contained in the wedge of land between East Hickory and Middle Hickory creeks. Hickory Creek has been accorded wilderness status. Therefore, please keep group sizes small; no mountain bikes or motorized vehicles are permitted.

Although roadless today, the area was not always so. Nearly every valley contains the bed of a logging railroad, while old skid roads and more recent jeep trails lace the hillsides. The area was logged by Wheeler and Dusenbury of Endeavor, starting around 1910. This company lumbered in Pennsylvania and New York for over a century, starting in 1837.

Instead of doing Hickory Creek as a long day hike, many people prefer to turn it into a backpack of two or more days. With just a daypack you can probably shave an hour or more off the hiking time, but backpackers will need the full seven hours on the trail. If you backpack, please camp at least 50 meters from the trail and from any stream. Practice minimal impact techniques.

The trailhead is at Hearts Content Picnic Area. Hearts Content is most easily reached from SR 3005 at a junction 10.1 miles from PA 62 at Tidioute and 11.4 miles from US 6 at Warren. Turn south on the Hearts Content-Sheffield Road (LR 61031). Another 3.7 miles brings you to the trailhead. Drinking water is available at the picnic area during the summer. Yellow paint blazes are used to mark the Hickory Creek Trail. Despite the length of the trail and some wet spots, you could get by with walking shoes if you are just day hiking.

The trail quickly traverses a red pine plantation and then crosses the road leading to Hearts Content. On the far side of the road it passes under the junction of two pole lines and joins the loop at 1.0 km (0.6 mile) from the start. Turn left through characteristically open woods. The very openness of the woods forces you to keep a sharp lookout for the paint blazes as the footway fades out frequently. But the footing is fairly even and the walking easy as you swing along, generally downhill.

You cross a woods road at 1.3 km (0.8 mile) and pass a spring to the right at 1.7 km (1.1 miles). At 2.4 km (1.5 miles) you cross a nameless tributary of Middle Hickory Creek on a log bridge, and immediately beyond you cross an old logging road.

Begin a gradual climb at 3.1 km (1.9 miles), and at the top pass through an open area abounding in ferns. The trail continues gently up and down as it follows the edge of the plateau. Trees along this stretch are black cherry, beech, maple, red oak and hemlock.

Just beyond 5.6 km (3.5 miles) you cross an old road and a dry watercourse and then bear left on another old road for a stretch. A large meadow along Coon Run is reached at 6.2 km (3.9 miles). You then cross a tributary of Coon and head downstream along the edge of the meadow.

The meadows along Coon Run offer the first opportunities for camping, and you will see several campsites along the trail. Cross Coon Run itself at 7.0 km (4.4 miles) and immediately cross the bed of a fine old logging railroad. Note the parallel depressions across the grade where the uncreosoted ties rotted in place. These depressions are one of the surest signs of an old railroad grade. Old railroad grades can be hard to identify, as most of them were never mapped. This one appears to have been standard gauge.

You now move upstream for 200 meters before diverging from the stream and starting the gradual climb into the next watershed. At 8.6 km (5.4 miles) cross an open swath leading to a meadow on your right and shortly jog left across an old road.

Cross a few streams at 9.3 km (5.8 miles) and then continue past a large meadow to your right. Among other trees growing here is yellow birch. Soon you are following an old logging railroad grade along Jacks Run. There are more opportunities for camping along this stream.

The ruins of an old logging camp can be found along Jacks Run. The camp was of unusual design in that it was all under one roof, like a railroad flat. Iron-

Meadow

work from school desks was found here. Was there once a small school in the midst of this now roadless area?

There are only a couple of stream crossings as the trail follows Jacks Run for about 1 km (0.6 mile). At the last crossing, turn right and start the gentle climb to the broad ridge between East and Middle Hickory creeks.

At a saddle 11.2 km (7.0 miles) in the ridge the trail switches to the far side and continues to climb, reaching the top of the hill at 11.9 km (7.4 miles). There should be some leaves-off views over the valley of East Hickory Creek from this section.

At 12.5 km (7.8 miles) cross a small stream, and at 13.3 km (8.3 miles) swing away from the edge of the ridge, cross another small stream, and start to climb again. Now swing right, along the

base of a slope, and climb among large boulders.

At 14.0 km (8.8 miles) you are back to an edge that drops off to the left. Cross a jeep trail at 14.6 km (9.1 miles), a small meadow at 15.2 km (9.5 miles), and another old railroad grade at 16.0 km (10.0 miles). These landmarks are followed by a woods road at 16.6 km (10.4 miles), and at 17.7 km (11.1 miles) you are back at the loop junction. Turn left, and it is 1.0 km (0.6 mile) back to the trailhead and your car.

Other hikes in the Hearts Content vicinity are to be found on the nearby Tanbark Trail and some shorter trails. Two circuit hikes using the Tanbark Trail are described in Hikes 19 and 21. A very short hike in the Hearts Content Scenic Area is described in Hike 17.

30

Tionesta Scenic Area

Distance: 7.9 km (4.9 miles)
Time: 3 hours
Rise: 113 meters (370 feet)
Highlights: Virgin timber; tornado swath; relics of the
  Petroleum Age
Maps: USGS 7½' Ludlow, Sheffield; Hiker's Guide to
  Allegheny National Forest, map 5

In 1934, with the help of the Pennsylvania Forestry Association, the United States Forest Service bought 1647 hectares (4,100 acres) of virgin timber southeast of Sheffield. This tract was divided into two parts of roughly equal size. The Tionesta Scenic Area is open to the public and is traversed by the North Country and Twin Lakes trails. The remainder of the area was designated the Tionesta Natural Area, which is used strictly for research to monitor the changes of a mature and unmanaged forest. A natural gas storage field is located beneath the area. Research carried out at Tionesta has found that hobblebush, the most common brush in the 1940s, vanished by the early 1950s. This change is attributed to heavy browsing by deer.

On the evening of 31 May 1985, a tornado cut a swath through the Tionesta Scenic Area, destroying much of it and causing the North Country Trail to be rerouted along a pipeline. As a result, this hike is now a car shuttle hike.

One trailhead is on PA 948, 5.3 miles south of the intersection with US 6 in

Sheffield. (Note that PA 948 ends in the village of Barnes and that you reach Sheffield on PA 666.) Leave one car along the highway near the North Country Trail sign or where Forestry Road (FR) 148 crosses Tionesta Creek, if you prefer. Drive back to Sheffield and turn right (east) on US 6. Drive 6.1 miles to the outskirts of Ludlow, turn right at a sign for Tionesta Scenic Area on South Hillside Street and in one block turn left on Water Street. Next, turn right on Scenic Drive, cross the railroad where this road becomes FR 133, which you will

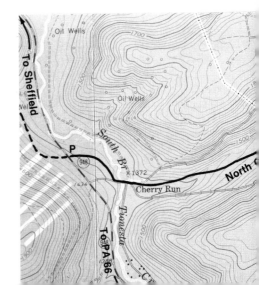

follow for 5.8 miles from US 6, avoiding a host of other roads along the way. Turn right on FR 133E for 1.2 miles more to the trailhead parking on the loop at the end of the road in the Tionesta Scenic Area. The car shuttle sounds formidable but there are a number of strategically placed Tionesta Scenic Area signs along the way and most of the alternative roads are not that tempting. The car shuttle takes about 50 minutes.

Due to many wet spots, hiking boots are strongly recommended.

The interpretive trail is no longer maintained so make your way as best you

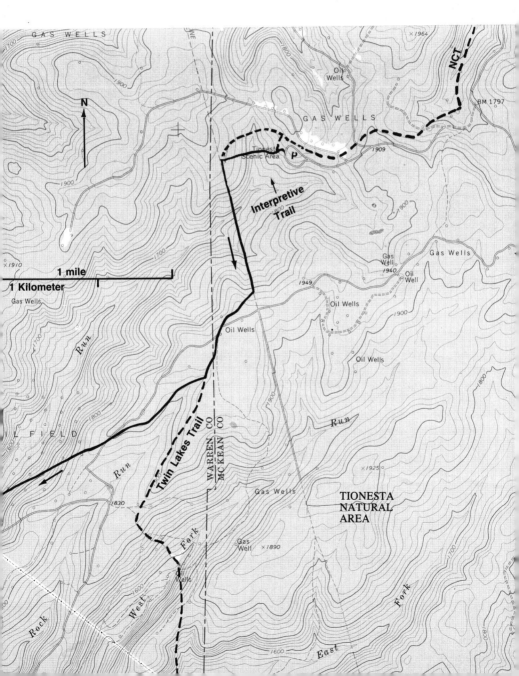

Damaged forest in Tionesta Scenic Area

can to the North Country Trail and turn left. Blue plastic rectangles are used to mark the North Country Trail.

Here you may hear a red-tailed hawk skimming the treetops, screaming again and again, adding a wild note to this primeval forest. Many of the largest trees are hemlocks. It seems curious that such large trees have such tiny cones. A hemlock cone is only the size of the end of your little finger. It contains winged seeds, each weighing only two or three milligrams.

At 0.8 km (0.5 miles) turn left along the pipeline through the swath of tornado damage. It is hard to imagine how strong were the forces of nature that produced all this destruction in just a minute or so as the funnel cloud moved by.

Cross the bridge over Cherry Run at the bottom of the valley and then climb the far side. As soon as you leave the tornado damage on the far side, start looking for a very obscure turn on the right. Turns on the NCT are marked with an "L" shaped blaze, with the base of the "L" pointing in the direction of the turn. Some of these turn blazes have the cross member at the top, making a "7" blaze instead. This turn doesn't seem to have either type of blaze. If you miss this turn you will reach a broken steel gate and a jeep road at the top of the hill. In any case, turn right at 1.8 km (1.1 miles) and follow the NCT along the edge of the tornado swath. Next, you pass an old oil well in a clearing and then jog right on a jeep road.

At 2.8 km (1.7 miles) you reach one of the major trail junctions in Allegheny National Forest. This one is with the blue-blazed Twin Lakes Trail. The somewhat confusing distance sign on the North Country Trail predates 1975, when this section was still the Tanbark Trail. The North Country Trail does not go to Hearts Content and it will be a lot more than 29 miles when the North Country Trail is finally extended to the Allegheny River, in spite of the sign.

At 3.2 km (2.0 miles) you cross a jeep road and soon the trail threads its way among large sandstone boulders. Every so often you encounter old pipes that once collected oil from wells now gone dry. Bear right on an old grade at 4.0 km (2.5 miles) and descend gently. The boundary of the Tionesta Scenic Area is marked by a display case at 4.5 km (2.8 miles). For a considerable stretch along this grade there were no plastic markers when I hiked it and I had to follow the old white paint blazes.

At 5.2 km (3.2 miles) you pass an old oil well. North Country Trail sticks to the south side of Cherry Run. At 5.7 km (3.5 miles) you cross a power line swath. At 7.3 km (4.5 miles) turn right on FR 148 and cross Tionesta Creek. I wish that the North Country Trail could follow this lovely stream and its stand of hemlocks for a greater distance. Turn right on the NCT and follow it out to PA 948 and your car.

31

Browns Run

Distance: 6.0 km (3.7 miles)
Time: 2 hours
Rise: 90 meters (300 feet)
Highlights: Evergreens; North Country Trail
Maps: USGS 7½' Cooksburg; state park map; Baker Trail
  maps

This is an easy hike in the more remote parts of Cook Forest State Park. All the stream crossings are bridged and the route follows old roads and railroad grades. The trade-off is that there are virtually no blazes. The required car shuttle is straightforward. This trail is almost entirely through a thick growth of hemlock and white pine. See Hike 23 for information on the history of Cook Forest State Park. Walking shoes are fine for this hike. This trail, coming from either direction, has a minimal amount of climbing.

Cook Forest State Park is on PA 36 about 15 miles north of exit 13 on I-80 at Brookville. Both trail heads are on the Vowinckel Road. The first is 4.0 miles north of PA 36 or 1.8 miles south of PA 66 at Vowinckel. Leave one car at a small area on the east side of the road. Then drive south for 3.0 miles on the Vowinckel Road and park at the Log Cabin Inn Nature Center, which is the same trail head as used for Hike 23.

To start the hike, cross the stone bridge over Toms Run and turn right on the combined Liggett and Baker trails. These trails follow the grade of the logging railroad that supplied the sawmill at

Cooksburg for so many years. The North Country Trail logo shows that the Baker Trail has been designated as part of this great but unfinished national scenic trail.

Soon you pass a signed junction with the Camp Trail which leads uphill left to the Ridge Campground. At 0.5 km (0.3 mile) you cross a wooden bridge which is typical of the care with which cross streams have been bridged on this trail.

Keep right on the Baker Trail at 0.8 km (0.5 mile) where the Corduroy Trail diverges to the left. Cross three more bridges of pressure-treated lumber before reaching 1.7 km (1.1 miles) where the Liggett Trail turns right and crosses Toms Run. Continue on the Baker and Brown Run trails.

At 2.3 km (1.4 miles) turn right off the old railroad grade and cross a bridge over Toms Run. Jog right on the unpaved Toms Run road for 30 meters and continue on an old road which makes a green tunnel through the evergreens. At 3.0 km (1.9 miles) you get your first look at Browns Run itself. Turn left at 3.5 km (2.2 miles), where the Deer Meadow Trail goes right, and

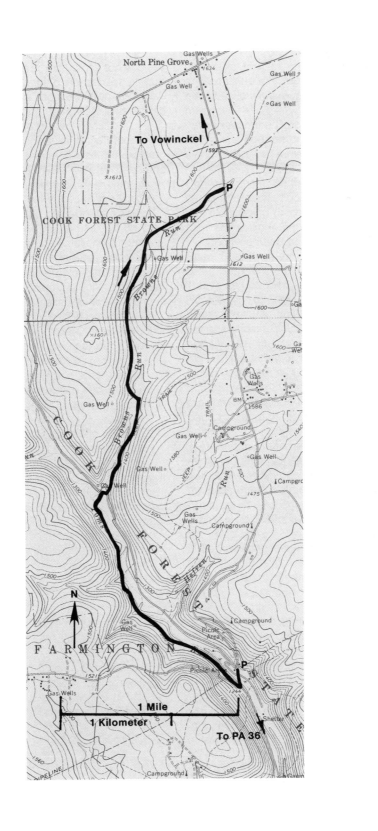

North Pine Grove

Gas Wells

Gas Well

×1634

Gas Well

To Vowinckel

/592

×1613

/600

P

COOK FOREST STATE PARK

Browns Run

/600

×1601

Gas Well

/1612

Gas Well

/600

Gas

/1600

C O O K

Browns Run

Gas Well

TRAIL

Gas Wells

BM

/1586

Campground

Ga

Gas Well

/1580

Gas Well

Campground

Gas Well

/1600

/500

F O R E

JEEP

Run

Campgro

Gas Well

/1475

Gas Wells

/500

Gas Wells

Campground

N

S T

Gas Well

/1300

Toms

Helen

Campground

Gas Well

Picnic Area

F A R M I N G T O N

/1521

Picnic Ar

P

/1244

Gas Wells

1 Mile

1 Kilometer

Shelter

To PA 36

/1560

PIPELINE

Campground

/500

North Country National Scenic Trail

cross a bridge over Browns Run. Then turn right on the Bridle Trail. Yes, this trail is designated for horses but I found little evidence of such usage. The trail continues through evergreens galore with occasional glimpses of Browns Run.

At 5.0 km (3.1 miles) bear left off the old railroad grade and follow some blue plastic markers across a bridge. Soon you return to the same old railroad grade, still following the blue markers. Keep right on the Baker and Browns Run trails at 5.3 km (3.3 miles) where the Bridle Trail diverges to the left. Cross several plank bridges and arrive at the paved Vowinckel Road. Turn left to reach the parking area.

Pittsburgh and
the Southwest

32

Wolf Creek Narrows

Distance: 2.4 km (1.5 miles)
Time: 50 minutes
Rise: 43 meters (140 feet)
Highlight: Spring wildflowers
Maps: USGS 7½' Slippery Rock; Western Pennsylvania
   Conservancy brochure map

Wolf Creek Narrows, near Slippery Rock in Butler County, is one of the more recent acquisitions of the Western Pennsylvania Conservancy. When I first visited the area, I had to cross a piece of private land, between the road and the Conservancy tract, that was open to Conservancy members only. Three months later, the Conservancy made another purchase so the trail to Wolf Creek Narrows Natural Area is now open to the public. Wolf Creek has its headwaters in Pine Swamp Natural Area, another Conservancy holding.

The big attraction of Wolf Creek Narrows is its wildflowers in late April and early May. The ground is carpeted with them. You also get the best views of the creek before the trees leaf out. Laying out trails in a new natural area is painful, since you can't avoid destroying some of the wildflowers you are trying to save. It has to be done however, since without established trails "horde paths" might well destroy even more.

The trailhead for Wolf Creek Narrows is 1.7 miles west of PA 258 in Slippery

Fiddleheads

Rock, on West Water Street. Cross the bridge over Wolf Creek and take the first left. Parking is permitted just inside the fringe of trees along the road, but please don't block the lane and don't park along the road. Ordinary walking shoes should be fine for this short hike.

To start, walk back across the bridge and turn left on the signed trail at the end of the bridge abutment. This trail takes you upstream along Wolf Creek into the bulk of the Natural Area. At 0.4 km (0.3 mile) you encounter the first white blazes. Keep a sharp eye out for the loop trail junction where you turn right and follow the trail across the bottom land to the base of the hill. Many of the best wildflowers are found on the south slope of the hill. Trees growing on the slope are black cherry, hemlock, beech, maple, basswood and black gum. In late April, abundant wildflowers are hepatica, mayapple and trillium.

At 1.0 km (0.6 mile) turn left above the narrows. Glimpses of Wolf Creek can be seen between the trees. Soon you reach the edge of the hill and descend to the creek, which runs on bedrock at this point. The trail continues

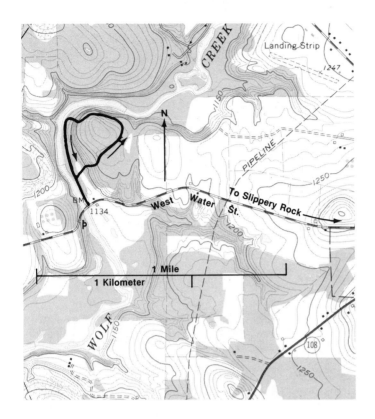

along the edge of the stream and under the hemlock, with views of the small limestone cliffs on the far side. At 1.9 km (1.2 miles) you close the loop trail and retrace your steps to your car.

The conservancy tract includes an area on the far side of Wolf Creek. It has no marked trails and can be reached only by fording the creek. The Jennings Nature Reserve, on the other side of Slippery Rock at the junction of PA 8 and PA 173, offers additional trails and wildflowers. (See Hike 34.)

33

Todd Sanctuary

Distance: 3.4 km (2.1 miles)
Time: 1½ hours
Rise: 75 meters (240 feet)
Highlights: Spring wildflowers; birds
Maps: USGS 7½' Freeport; Nature Trail map

Todd Sanctuary consists of 65 hectares (160 acres) along Watson Run in the southeast corner of Butler County. Owned and operated by the Audubon Society of Western Pennsylvania, it is named for the late W.E. Clyde Todd, curator of the bird section in the Carnegie Museum of Natural History. Todd spent his boyhood summers near here over 70 years ago and began a detailed study of the bird population. At least 214 species of birds have been observed here, so be sure to bring your binoculars. Todd Sanctuary dates back to 1942, making it one of the first natural areas to be preserved in the vicinity of Pittsburgh.

This delightful short hike is designed to take you through all the different habitats in the sanctuary. It would be particularly suitable for small children as there are lots of things to see and discover, including some blackberries in season. There are also many opportunities to shorten the hike. Spring wildflowers include bloodroot, trailing arbutus, trillium, spring beauty, Dutchman's-breeches and forget-me-not. The best displays are in the bottom lands along Watson Run. The trails are excellent, so ordinary walking shoes are fine; insects are not a real problem.

To reach Todd Sanctuary from Pittsburgh, take new PA 28 and turn north on PA 356. In 1.0 mile turn east on Monroe Road, across from Cinema 356 and just before Tom Bonello's Family Restaurant. After crossing the railroad tracks and going up a steep hill, bear right at a fork in the road. This is Kepple Road, which takes you past a golf course to reach the Todd Sanctuary sign, 3.0 miles from PA 356. Turn right into the parking lot.

The hike starts at the bulletin board in the corner of the parking lot. Follow the trail and turn right on the road paralleling Knixon's Run. After 100 meters turn left at McCray Crossing, a footbridge over Hesselgesser's Run, to the cabin where you will usually find a naturalist or two in residence. A recycled birdhouse or other receptacle at the cabin will receive your contribution, which is needed for the sanctuary's support. A guest register is maintained here and there are usually several informal exhibits. Drinking water is available.

Bear right around the cabin and then go left on the white blazed Loop Trail.

You soon turn left where the Warbler Trail goes ahead. At 0.6 km (0.4 mile) you pass an old limestone quarry to the left of the trail, where much of the stone to build the cabin was obtained. Bear left where the Warbler Trail comes in from the right. At 0.9 km (0.6 mile) you cross Watson Run on stepping stones, just before the Indian Pipe Trail goes off to the right.

Next, bear left on the Loop Trail (the Pond Trail goes ahead). Soon you emerge at the edge of the pond, which was created in 1969 to attract migrating water birds. As you continue through the meadow around the pond, there is a large white farmhouse to your left. This is the farmhouse, belonging to his grandfather, where W.E. Clyde Todd spent his boyhood summers.

Trees along the Loop Trail are shingle oak, red oak, white oak, crab apple, black gum, scotch pine, dogwood, black cherry and hemlock. At 1.6 km

(1.0 mile) turn left on the Loop Trail where the Meadow Trail goes ahead, and at 1.9 km (1.2 miles) you again go left on the Loop Trail where the Poly-pody Trail goes right. Finally at 2.5 km (1.6 miles) bear left on the Loop Trail where the Indian Pipe Trail goes right. Pass among some large boulders and you get a view across Watson Run from the brink of a cliff. There is no guard rail, so be careful. Inspiration Point makes a good lunch stop.

Turn north through the hemlock at the edge of the cliff. At 2.9 km (1.8 miles) turn left and descend to the Ravine Trail on which you turn right. (The Ravine Trail shares the narrow stream bottom with Watson Run, so at times of high water you would do better to stick to the Loop Trail.)

Cross Watson Run as best you can, and at 3.2 km (2.0 miles) there is an old mill site to the right of the trail. The mill was located at the confluence of Watson

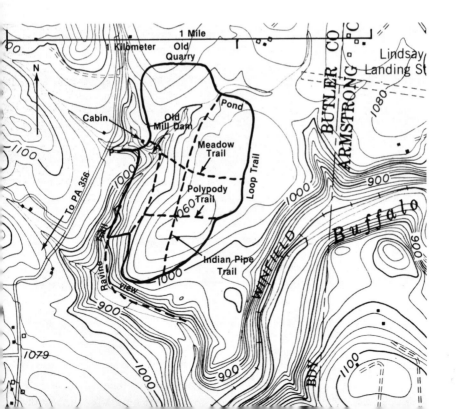

Goldenrod

and Hesselgesser runs. All that remains is part of the stone dam on the far side, but this is certainly one of the gems of Todd Sanctuary. Back on the trail, McCray Crossing is just around the bend. From here you retrace your steps to the parking lot or drop in at the cabin again.

The only other hike of any length descends Watson Run on the Ravine Trail to the edge of the Todd property. The private land beyond is closed to hikers, so you must retrace your steps.

Jennings Environmental Education Center

Distance: 3.5 km (2.2 miles)
Time: 1¼ hours
Rise: 75 meters (240 feet)
Highlights: Prairie wildflowers; massasauga rattlesnakes
Maps: USGS 7½' Slippery Rock; park map

Although most of Pennsylvania was heavily wooded at the time of settlement, there were a few bits of prairie, remnants from a period of higher temperatures about 4000 years ago when the tall grass prairies expanded to the east. Here, on the beach of glacial Lake Edmund, was one of them. Found here are plants of western prairies, particularly the blazing star, which blooms in late July and early August, and is worth a special trip. Many other wildflowers, including woodland varieties, also occur at Jennings. So a visit any time from early spring to fall will likely find something in bloom. In all, 386 species of plants have been observed at Jennings. The more people look, the more they find.

The occurrence of the blazing star on a tract of only three acres was recognized by Dr. Otto E. Jennings, a botanist and educator. Dr. Jennings succeeded in getting the Western Pennsylvania Conservancy to purchase this 125 hectares (310 acres) tract containing the tiny relict prairie. By clearing portions of the adjacent woodland, the prairie has since been expanded to about 12 hectares (30 acres). The bulk of the area remains wooded. The Western Pennsylvania Conservancy transferred the area to public ownership and it is now operated by the Bureau of State Parks as an environmental education center.

The center is also home to the massasauga rattlesnake. The massasauga is shorter than the timber rattlesnake, prefers to live in swamps and is shy and retiring. Stay on the established trails so you won't meet the massasauga unexpectedly. Should you be lucky enough to spot this elusive reptile, observe it from a distance with binoculars or a telephoto lens. The massasauga is endangered in Pennsylvania and consequently protected.

Jennings is located at the junction of PA 8, PA 173 and PA 528, about twelve miles north of Butler, four miles south of Slippery Rock and adjacent to the boundary of Moraine State Park. You can park in either of the lots at Jennings but the one on the north side of PA 528 adjacent to the prairie is more convenient for this hike. The trails at Jennings have been hardened in recent years to reduce the amount of mud so good walking shoes are fine for this hike.

To start your hike, walk between the pillars marking the entrance to the Blazing Star Trail. Note the flowing or artesian well to the right of these pillars. After only 65 meters of this graveled path you enter the prairie at the junction of the Massasauga Trail, on which you will return at the end of your hike. Look here for the blazing star. Note the evidence of man-made fire required to keep the forest from returning. Shortly, you pass the Prairie Loop Trail on your right, which you could take to lengthen your stay among the prairie wildflowers. The loop would add only 370 meters to your hike. At the far side of the prairie bear right on the Deer Trail. Trail junc-

tions are all signed at Jennings. At 0.6 km (0.4 mile) bear right on the Oakwoods Trail.

You will pass several old pits to the left of the trail. Just what was sought here remains a mystery. Recent excavation failed to find anything of value. Speculation now centers on clay for a long-gone pottery. To the right of the trail, three rows of daffodils give seasonal evidence of a vanished homestead.

At 1.4 km (0.9 mile) the trail follows an old fence marking the boundary of private land. Shagbark hickory, shingle oak, white oak and black cherry are frequent trees along this section. The trail

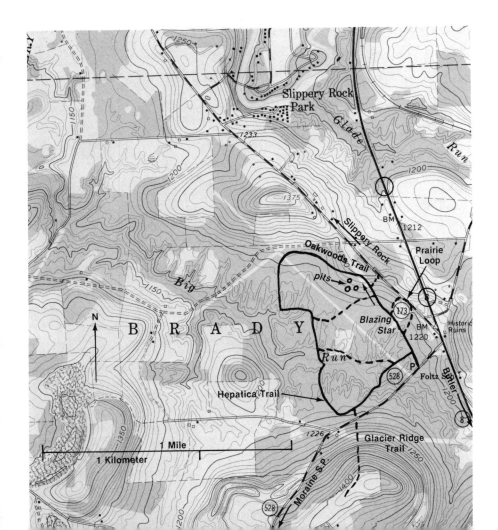

follows along a small stream before crossing it on a bridge.

Just after rounding a corner of private land the old field trail diverges to the left. Continue along the fence and descend into the bottoms bordering Big Run and cross a bridge over a wet area. At 2.4 km (1.5 miles) turn right on Hepatica Trail and cross Big Run on another bridge.

Beyond Big Run the Hepatica Trail climbs up the stream bank. It then reaches the junction with the Glacier Ridge Trail. The Glacier Ridge Trail has been rebuilt and now proceeds southwest through Moraine State Park and has been designated as part of the North Country National Scenic Trail.

Turn left on the Glacier Ridge Trail. Note the remains of a split rail fence to the left of the trail. After recrossing Big Run look for gabions (wire baskets filled with rocks) used to stabilize the stream bank. At 3.2 km (2.0 miles) turn right on the Massasauga Trail, which passes a picnic pavilion and continues along the edge of the prairie to a junction with the Blazing Star Trail. Turn right and it is just a few steps to the parking lot.

There are further opportunities for walking at Jennings. This hike has bypassed a number of trails that could be used to truncate or extend it. To the south of PA 528, a circuit hike can be made on the Old Mill, Black Cherry and Ridge Trails. Just across PA 8 is the "Old Stone House," a replica of a stage coach inn dating from the 1820s where guests, who ranged from counterfeiters to the Marquis de Lafayette, were required to remove their boots in bed but were promised that there would be no more than five people per bed.

Drinking from an artesian well

35

Beechwood Nature Trails

Distance: 4.0 km (2.5 miles)
Time: 1¾ hours
Rise: 115 meters (380 feet)
Highlight: A pleasant walk
Maps: USGS 7½' Glenshaw; Nature Reserve map (available at Evans Nature Center)

Beechwood Farms is a small nature reserve within the Pittsburgh metropolitan area owned by the Western Pennsylvania Conservancy and operated by the Western Pennsylvania Audubon Society. Because of its many steep-walled valleys, Pittsburgh has an abundance of undeveloped land that frequently serves as a refuge for wildlife. Beechwood, a tract of upland once operated as a dairy farm, is being permitted to return to its natural state.

Beechwood Farms can be reached from exit 4 on the Pennsylvania Turnpike. Go south on PA 8 for 3.0 miles and then turn left on the Green Belt, which at this point is Harts Run Road. The Green Belt is one of several systems of roads that encircle Pittsburgh. Follow the Green Belt for 3.7 miles and then turn right on the Dorseyville Road at a stop sign. Another 0.3 mile brings you to the Beechwood parking lot, just across from the Fox Chapel fire department.

Walking shoes are fine for this short hike. Don't forget your binoculars for a little birding.

On my most recent visit to Beechwood I was delighted to find that much of the poison ivy has been replaced by goldenrod. Poison ivy no longer presents the hazard at Beechwood that it did some years ago.

Dogs are prohibited on the trails at Beechwood. Leave Rover at home so you won't have to lock him in your car. If the Evans Nature Center is open, visitors should register. There are plenty of exhibits, and you can go down the stairs to the basement where there are restrooms and then use the back door to reach the trails.

Starting at the trailhead sign, bear right on a mowed path through the meadow, which affords a view of the farm pond. Then turn right at the edge of the woods and continue ahead on the Oak Forest Trail, which is yellow-blazed. The Oak Forest Trail is crossed and then recrossed by a bridle trail.

Continue through woods which contain dogwood and shadbush as well as oak. This trail makes a close approach to Harts Run Road, which you can see through the trees even with the leaves on.

At 0.6 km (0.4 mile) turn right on the

Mighty oaks

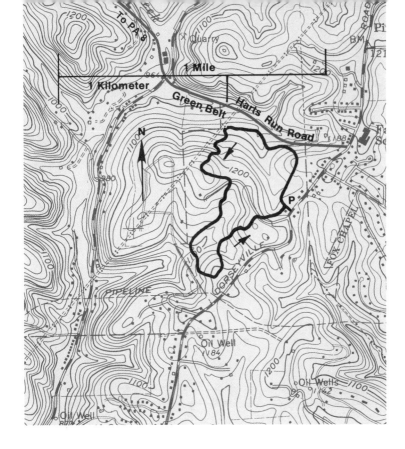

yellow-blazed Spring Hollow Walk. Descend next to an old eroded road. Cross Harts Run and then start the climb back to the uplands.

At 0.8 km (0.5 mile) continue on the white-blazed Woodland Trail, which switchbacks up the hill. It comes very close to a powerline swath at one point. Turn left at the top of the hill and descend to a meadow.

Turn right on Meadow View Trail at 1.6 km (1.0 mile) and cross a private driveway; then turn right on Pine Hollow Trail at 1.9 km (1.2 miles). You soon enter the woods and cross Beechwood Run on what was an old driveway and is now a red-blazed bridle path.

Cross an old dam at 2.4 km (1.5 miles) which has completely silted in. Then climb through an evergreen plan-

tation. Red pine, then white pine, larch and finally a band of Norway spruce is encountered on the way down this hill. Cross the bridle trail where it follows a poleline, then turn right on Meadow View Trail at 3.5 km (2.2 miles). You pass a number of mulberry trees, always a favorite of fruit-eating birds. Shortly, turn left for Meadow View Lookout, only 40 meters down the side trail, which provides a view across the meadows of Beechwood Farms.

Back on the Meadow View Trail, you cross a private drive and then turn right on Spring Hollow Walk. Soon you are back at the Evans Nature Center and your car.

More trails are available at nearby Hartwood Park, a county regional park.

36

Harrison Hills Park

In-and-out distance: 4.0 km (2.5 miles)
Time: 1½ hours
Rise: 115 meters (380 feet)
Highlights: Views; Rachel Carson Trail
Maps: USGS 7½' Freeport; Rachel Carson Trail maps
(available from American Youth Hostels Pittsburgh Council)

Harrison Hills Park is in the extreme northeast corner of Allegheny County on the bluffs above the Allegheny River. In 1949, members of the newly-formed Pittsburgh Council of the American Youth Hostels were on a canoe trip; the cliffs inspired them to build a cross-country foot trail from Pittsburgh to Cook Forest State Park. The trail was named after Horace Forbes Baker, who established the Pittsburgh Council shortly before his death. Originally, the Baker Trail started at the Highland Park bridge over the Allegheny. Rapid development soon forced abandonment of all 40 kilometers (25 miles) of the trail in Allegheny County.

An attempt was made in the early seventies to salvage parts of the original Baker Trail and weld them into a new trail across northern Allegheny County. This trail passes close to the birthplace of Rachel Carson, the famous environmentalist. Rachel Carson is known best for her books, *The Sea Around Us* (1951) and *Silent Spring* (1962). The latter warned of the dangers of herbicides and pesticides, particularly DDT.

A 53 kilometer (33 miles) trail was fi-

nally blazed, stretching from North Park to Harrison Hills, mostly on private land. This hike takes you along one of the few sections on public land. It is also part of the original Baker Trail.

Harrison Hills Park can be reached only from old PA 28. It is on the east side of the highway, north of Birdville and about half a mile beyond the traffic lights at the Highlands Mall. Just inside the park entrance take the left fork of the road and follow it to its end in a parking lot (one of several near the cliffs), about 0.9 mile from the highway. Drinking water and restrooms are available at the picnic area. There is some poison ivy along the trail, and the cliffs are unforgiving. Keep a tight hold on children and dogs. Walking shoes are fine despite some wet places.

From the parking lot, head across the open area past the picnic shelter to a break in the trees that provides a view across the Allegheny into Westmoreland County. Then turn left and pick up the yellow blazes of the Rachel Carson Trail where it heads into the woods passing the Michael Watts Memorial Overlook. Mr. Watts was a native of Pittsburgh who worked to restore clean water to the rivers and streams of western Pennsylvania. The trail pops back into the picnic area again before committing itself to the woods.

Generally the path you want is the one closest to the edge of the cliffs. Beware of some unmarked trails, which are reputed to descend steeply all the way to the river. At 0.7 km (0.4 mile) you cross a stream, which you can hear cascading over the cliff. There is a view to the right of the trail at the brink of the cliff. Soon a mowed path comes in from the left, and you should bear right on it.

Shortly, another side stream is encountered. Take the first path leaving the mowed path, cross the stream and continue along the edge. At 1.3 km (0.8 mile) there is a view of the PA 356 bridge at Freeport. Basswood trees and serviceberries grow right at the brink. There are two picnic tables chained to a tree at this point. Descend and continue

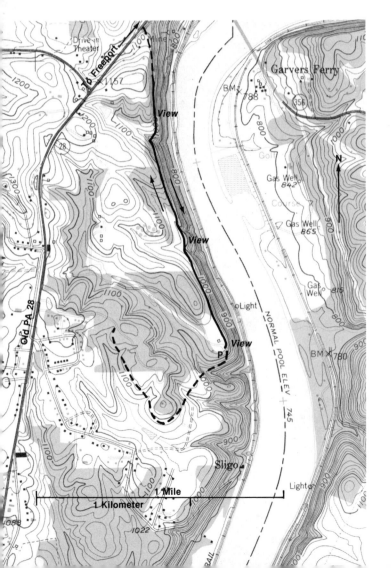

View of Allegheny River

north below the edge of the bluffs, cross a stream in a deep ravine at 1.5 km (0.9 mile) and then climb back to the top of the hill. You reach a walled spring at 1.9 km (1.2 miles). Continue until the trail emerges on a gravel road. From here it crosses backyards, so turn and retrace your steps to your car.

Other hiking opportunities can be found at nearby Todd Sanctuary (Hike 33).

37

Raccoon Creek Wildflower Reserve

Distance: 3.9 km (2.4 miles)
Time: 1½ hours
Rise: 30 meters (100 feet)
Highlight: Wildflowers
Maps: USGS 7½' Aliquippa, Clinton; state park map

Raccoon Creek State Park is located in Beaver County, about 25 miles west of Pittsburgh. It is a large park by Pennsylvania standards and was established by the National Park Service back in the Great Depression through the acquisition of submarginal farm land. Ruins of some of these farms can still be found in the undeveloped western portions of the park. Despite its name, most of the park occupies the valley of Traverse Creek. This hike is in the only part of the park on Raccoon Creek. This is the small portion east of US 30, set aside as a wildflower reserve and originally purchased by the Western Pennsylvania Conservancy. It was transferred to the state in 1971.

The only entrance to the wildflower reserve is from US 30, about 3 miles west of Clinton. Pets are not permitted on the trails of the wildflower reserve. Drive through the evergreen plantation and park. If time permits—and this is a short, easy hike—stop in at the nature center. The trails might be a little muddy but ordinary walking shoes should be fine. The best time to visit Raccoon Creek for spring wildflowers is the second week of May.

The hike starts on the Jennings Trail

at the far end of the parking area. The Jennings Trail has the greatest variety of plant life, and it also intersects many other trails, permitting you to vary or truncate the hike. Moving along the Jennings Trail, you climb a small hill and then circle around Hungerford Cabin. Hungerford was a cartoonist for the *Pittsburgh Press and Post Gazette*, and this cabin was his second home. Second homes were modest in those days. Beyond the clearing, use the switchbacks to descend the slope. At 0.4 km (0.3 mile) the Deer Trail goes left and shortly the Big Maple Trail does the same. Along this section you can see woodland wildflowers such as mayapples and hepatica. These wildflowers must grow and bloom in the few short weeks of spring before the deciduous trees leaf out. At 0.6 km (0.4 mile) the trail crosses a small stream and at 0.8 km (0.5 mile) it reaches the top of a low cliff. Bear left and descend the recently rebuilt steps. You may notice some poison ivy along the trail.

In these bottom lands look for trillium and Virginia bluebell. Also note the wood duck box on a post in the slough. There are a great many bird boxes installed in the wildflower reserve. They

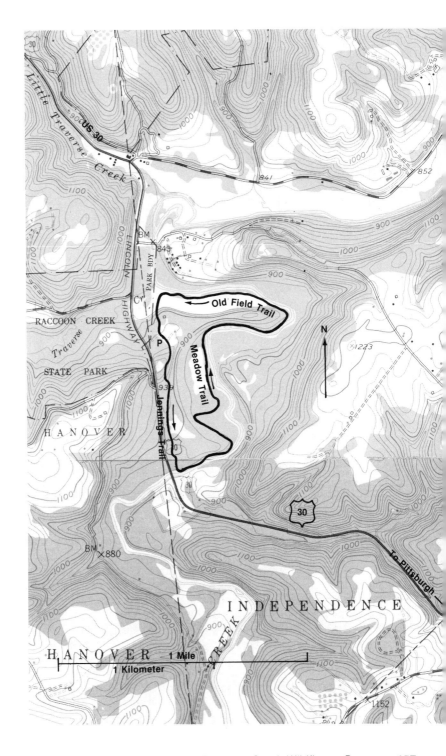

Jack-in-the-Pulpit

are all worth a hard look, as they may have interesting tenants. Different species of trees grow here in the bottom land. Largest of these is the sycamore with its peeling light-colored bark. The silence on the bottom land is frequently broken by jets taking off from the Greater Pittsburgh Airport.

The Jennings Trail hugs the base of the upland and passes the Big Oak (now dead) shown on the park map. At 1.4 km (0.9 mile) you turn full right on the Old Wagon Road Trail. The Old Wagon Road Trail takes you out onto the bottom land towards Raccoon Creek. At 1.6 km (1.0 mile) you bear left on the Meadow Trail and enter a large meadow on the bottom land. The open meadow is a very different environment. Here one may find wildflowers blooming in the summer and fall. Bird boxes may harbor the rare eastern bluebird. Ignore the Hickory Trail.

At 2.1 km (1.3 miles) turn right on the Jennings Trail again, which lies between the base of the cliffs and Raccoon Creek. Note the large tulip trees growing on the bottom land. Here the Beaver Trail makes an optional loop to the right.

At 2.7 km (1.6 miles) you turn right on the Old Field Trail at the junction with the Audubon Trail. This trail takes you back to the creek and then between the creek and the old field. Keep left at 2.8 km (1.7 miles) at an obscure trail junction, ignore a cutoff trail and bear right at a trail junction. The Travis Trail makes another optional loop to the right. Then circle back to a junction with the Henrici Trail at 3.7 km (2.3 miles). (Henrici was an outdoor writer from Sewickly.) Turn right and climb back up the hill. At the top, bear right on the road. The parking lot is visible ahead.

It is a scandal that the hiking opportunities in this large park are so limited. The western portion of the park could easily contain a nice circuit hike.

38

McConnells Mill State Park

Distance: 5.2 km (3.2 miles)
Time: 2 hours
Rise: 103 meters (340 feet)
Highlights: Gorge; waterfalls; rapids; wildflowers; old mill;
  covered bridge
Maps: USGS 7½' Portersville; state park map

Geologically, the gorge of Slippery Rock Creek is quite recent, dating only from the last ice age. Before the ice age, Slippery Rock and Muddy creeks both flowed northwest to the St. Lawrence River. But with their way blocked by the continental ice sheet, large lakes formed in the valleys of the creeks. As the ice began to retreat, glacial Lake Arthur found a new outlet here, and the enormous flow of meltwater cut this gorge in only a few thousand years. Today, Slippery Rock Creek flows to the Ohio, and its gorge has become one of the few unspoiled hemlock ravines in the western part of the state. Twelve species of fern are found at McConnells Mill State Park, more than anywhere else in western Pennsylvania.

McConnells Mill State Park is about 40 miles north of Pittsburgh, just 0.3 mile west of the junction of US 422 with US 19 and 1.7 miles west of Exit 29 on I-79. Turn south off US 422, and it is another 0.7 mile to the parking lot at the Johnson Road junction where this hike begins. In driving south from US 422, you cross two of the sites where glacial Lake Arthur drained into Slippery Rock Gorge.

Good walking shoes are adequate for this hike which is best avoided in winter, as seep springs coat the rocks with ice making footing extremely treacherous. The spring wildflowers are usually at their peak around the third week in May.

To start your hike, walk north along the road about 100 meters to the Alpha Pass trailhead. A small stream flows over the edge of the Homewood Sandstone here, creating a small waterfall. This is one of the sites where glacial Lake Arthur drained its torrent into the gorge. At that time the ground here would have shaken under your feet. Head down the steep, but short, Alpha Pass Trail and reach the trail along the creek in another 100 meters. This trail is marked with orange paint blazes of irregular size and shape. There are several opportunities here to view the rapids in Slippery Rock Creek from the large blocks of sandstone that have slid down the side of the gorge.

Turn left and head downstream on this rough trail. At 0.5 km (0.3 mile) you pass a junction with the trail you will use at the end of your hike. Continue downstream on a smoother trail. Note the sizeable hemlocks that grow in the gorge. The evergreen shrub growing on some of the boulders is American yew. At 1.0 km (0.6 mile) you arrive at McConnells Mill. In the nineteenth century this wild and rugged location was valued not for its beauty but for its energy. When Thomas McConnell modernized his newly purchased mill in 1875, water power was still holding its own against steam. The mill was run by turbines rather than a water wheel, making it "one of the most modern in the century." This mill is still in operating order and on occasion is opened to the public. The mill and adjacent property were obtained by the Western Pennsylvania Conservancy and later conveyed to the state. Just beyond the mill is a covered bridge dating from 1874. You will return across this bridge, so pass it by for now and continue on the self-guiding Kildoo Nature Trail. The Kildoo Trail is paved! Enjoy it while you can, for there is

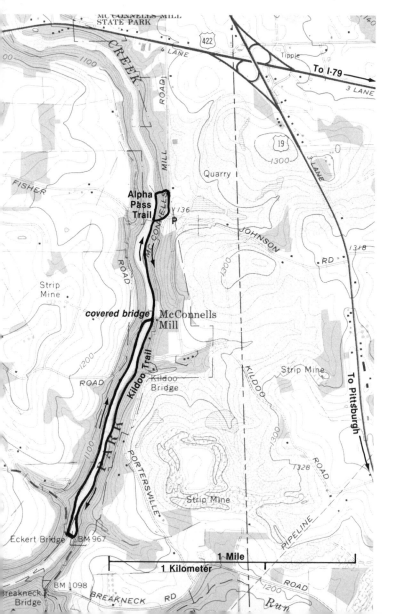

Covered Bridge

plenty of rough trail ahead with rocks and mud. Signs here bear the logo of the North Country National Scenic Trail. When completed the North Country Trail will run from New York state to North Dakota.

McConnells was not the only mill to use Slippery Rock Creek. At post 7 look for the ruins of another mill. At 1.4 km (0.9 mile) you cross a footbridge over Kildoo Creek. Here you leave the pavement behind and continue on rough trail. Keep watch just beyond here for millstones from an abandoned grist mill.

You reach the Eckert Bridge at 2.7 km (1.7 miles). The road is gated off at the west end of the Eckert Bridge. Cross this bridge and turn right at the far side on the return trail. Note the millstone mounted on a pedestal just beyond the bridge. By far the largest part of McConnells Mill State Park lies downstream from the Eckert Bridge. A recently built section of the North Country Trail (Hike 40) now connects the bridge with Hell's Hollow Trail.

Moving upstream you pass repeated displays of white and red trillium in season. Elsewhere trillium is rare. But when conditions are right, trillium may be locally abundant. This trail is much less used than the Kildoo and you may well experience moments when you seem to be alone in the gorge.

At 4.3 km (2.7 miles) you turn right and wait your chance to cross the covered bridge. Auto traffic is one way at a time on the bridge, and you may have to take the bridge on the run when the traffic changes direction. This brings you back to the mill for one last look and a drink at the fountain.

If the traffic is very light, follow the road back to the parking lot. It is an easy climb and passes between house-sized blocks of sandstone. If traffic is at its usual heavy level, head upstream along the trail and at 5.0 km (3.1 miles) turn right at the sign to the parking lot. The climb is steep but short, and you are soon back to your car.

Other attractions in McConnells Mill State Park are Cleland Rock and Hell's Hollow Trail. Cleland Rock provides views of Slippery Rock Gorge and is reached from Breakneck Bridge Road. Hell's Hollow Trail leads to a waterfall and an old iron furnace and is located on the west side of the park.

Glacier Ridge Trail

Distance: 6.6 km (4.1 miles)
Time: 2¼ hours
Rise: 65 meters (220 feet)
Highlights: North Country National Scenic Trail
Maps: USGS 7½' Prospect, Slippery Rock; Moraine State Park
map

This section of the Glacier Ridge Trail follows a corridor of state park land along PA 528 that was purchased with the express intention of connecting Moraine State Park and Jennings Environmental Education Center with a foot trail. The Glacier Ridge Trail has since been designated as a portion of the North Country National Scenic Trail. Such foresight does not always prevail. Moraine State Park is not connected with nearby McConnells Mill State Park. One of the challenges of trail development would be to connect these two parks by foot trail. For example, does the grade of the Western Allegheny Railroad follow Muddy Creek under the I-79 bridge? If so, it would make an ideal route across I-79 for the North Country Trail. Another challenge would be a backpack trail around Moraine Lake. Such a trail would be about 60 km (37 miles) long. Oil Creek State Park has such a trail. (See Hikes 48 and 50.) Why not Moraine? As with Oil Creek, it would be up to volunteers to scout, build and maintain these trails.

This is a car shuttle hike. First drive to Jennings Environmental Education Center at the junction of PA 8, PA 173 and

PA 528. This is the same trailhead as Hike 34. Park one car here in either of the lots at Jennings. Then drive south on PA 528 for 3.2 miles and park along the road opposite the road to a boat launch area. This is the same trailhead as Hike 42. Walking shoes should be fine for this short hike although there are some wet spots.

Follow the obvious path to the left of the road to the boat launch. The trail is marked with blue blazes but the trail follows a mowed path to the far side of West Liberty Road. Cross the remains of a bridge and proceed across a meadow which is a reclaimed strip mine. There are occasional blue blazes on wooden posts. The trail swings back to the edge of PA 528 at 650 meters and then climbs along a pole line. You reach the top of the hill at 1.0 km (0.6 mile). Next, the trail passes through an old apple orchard and at 1.4 km (0.9 mile) it crosses the paved Barkley Road.

Continue along the pole line and pass more old apple trees. Few, if any, bear any apples but such old orchards are good places to see a variety of birds. Cross a gravel road at 1.7 km (1.1 miles) and the paved West Liberty Road

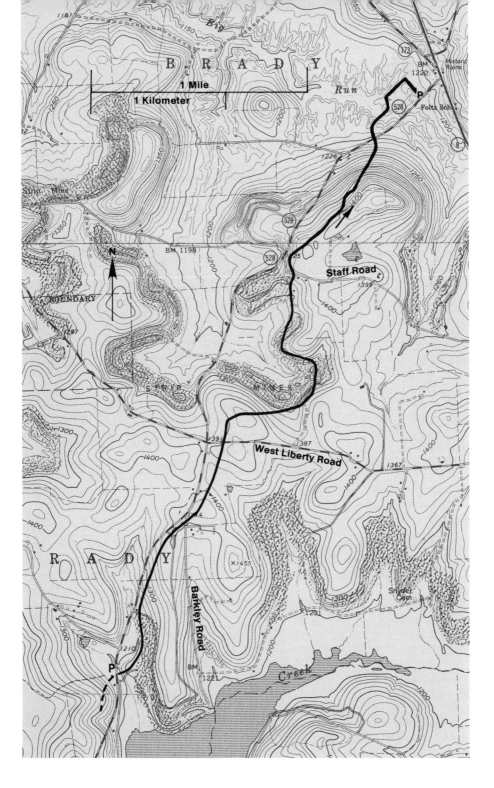

View towards Moraine Park

at 2.0 km (1.3 miles). PA 528 is just to the left. Continue along the pole line to 2.4 km (1.5 miles) where you turn right into the woods.

Cross a few old grades followed by a stream and then a dry stream bed. At 3.1 km (1.9 miles) there is a junction with a mysterious yellow-blazed trail that goes to the right. This trail is not shown on any map nor did the park office have any information on it.

Next the trail enters an extensive open area which is another reclaimed strip mine. The mine has been planted with white pine that seems to be thriving

so that in a few years there will be an abundance of trees to blaze as well as to shade your way, but for the moment blazes are few. Concentrate on the footway. Near 3.8 km (2.3 miles) you again get a mowed path to follow. At 4.1 km (2.5 miles) there is an obscure left turn into the woods. The only markings are the faded blue blazes on a post stuck in the ground. Pass through some red pine and find some more blazes. The trail then follows the border of a marsh (formerly a pond) and crosses the outlet. You pass a house to the right and some more red pine. The trail emerges at a gravel road, but turns left into the woods without crossing.

Shortly beyond at 4.6 km (2.8 miles) jog left across paved Staff Road. Climb the bank and continue through a patch of young sassafras. At 5.2 km (3.2 miles) an unmarked trail comes in from the right. Cross a pole line and PA 528 to enter Jennings Environmental Education Center. Turn right at 5.9 km (3.7 miles) where the Hepatica Trail comes in from the left. Note the old split rail fence just beyond, which is most visible on your left.

Cross Big Run on a footbridge and turn right on the Massasauga Trail at 6.4 km (4.0 miles). Turn right on the Blazing Star Trail which leads immediately to the north parking lot at Jennings.

A nearby hiking opportunity is Hike 34 which takes you on a tour of the prairie and other habitats at Jennings.

How is the North Country Trail to proceed from here? It is a considerable distance to S. G. L. 95 which is fragmented, and a lot farther to S. G. L. 283 along the Clarion River where the Western Pennsylvania Conservancy has bought land.

Slippery Rock Gorge Trail

Distance: 9.9 km (6.1 miles)
Time: 4½ hours
Rise: 245 meters (800 feet)
Highlights: Wildflowers; wild gorge; big trees
Maps: USGS 7½' Portersville; special trail map from park office

This portion of the North Country National Scenic Trail was built as a result of a campfire at Tamarack Fire Tower in Sproul State Forest in August 1990. Sitting around the fire, members of Keystone Trails Trail Care Team discussed the difficulty of finding significant trail projects in the western part of the state. It was decided to build a trail through the inaccessible part of McConnells Mill State Park from Eckert Bridge to Hell's Hollow. There already was a corridor of state park land down Slippery Rock Creek and up Hell Run.

Under leadership of the Shenango Outing Club and friends, the project took off. A route was explored, flagged and approved. The first work trip started in from Hell's Hollow in September 1991. A great deal of sidehill construction was required. Sidehill work is done with a tool called a Pulaski. Named for a forester, a Pulaski consists of an axe blade on one side and a hoe or adz on the other at the end of a pick handle. The operator uses the hoe to dig away the ground until a root is struck. The axe blade is then used to chop through the root.

The trail that resulted from three years of work is not an easy one. The Gorge Trail was formally opened 30 April 1994.

Apart from several intense climbs there are a lot of ups and downs along the way. At places the footway is narrow and you must watch your footing to avoid stepping off onto steep slopes. Wear your hiking boots for their added traction, and for the many seeps and wet spots along the way.

Slippery Rock Gorge was created in the last ice age when glacial Lake Arthur found a new outlet here. The enormous flow of meltwater cut this gorge in only a few thousand years. Consequently, the gorge is still changing on even our human time scale, as several recent landslides show.

The number of rock layers in the gorge contributes to its variety of soils, and its many seeps mean wet and dry sites alternate along the trail. At least sixty-nine species of wildflowers have been identified, making spring an excellent time for this hike. Fall colors make that season a strong second choice, but avoid the Gorge Trail in winter when ice may lurk beneath a veneer of snow. Wildflowers include white and red trillium, jack-in-the- pulpit, wild azalea, mayapple and blue phlox.

This is not a circuit hike; it requires a car shuttle. It should not be your first hike.

Small Falls on Hell Run

From exit 28 on I-79 drive west on PA 488 through Portersville for a total of 4.3 miles. Then turn right on Heinz Camp Road for 4.7 miles, crossing Slippery Rock Creek on the Armstrong Bridge. Lastly, turn right on Shaffer Road for just 0.1 mile to Hell's Hollow Falls parking lot. Leave one car here.

To reach Eckert Bridge and the start of this hike, turn right on Shaffer Road. After 0.5 mile, turn right on Fairview School Road. Follow this road for 2.6 miles and turn right on McConnells Mill Road, which you follow for 2.0 miles. Cross Slippery Rock Creek on the covered bridge. Then turn right on a dirt road that takes you up the side of the valley. Continue ahead at the top of the hill to Cheeseman Road. Turn right and follow Cheeseman Road downhill past a partial barricade to Eckert Bridge. Park here and begin your hike at the far side of Slippery Rock Creek.

Your hike starts at an old millstone mounted on a pedestal. Rectangular blue paint blazes mark the trail. This hike is laid out with the most strenuous sections of the Gorge Trail first. There is a fair amount of poison ivy along this first section. The trail is rocky and has lots of ups and downs. It closely follows Slippery Rock Creek, affording you a chance to watch kayaks if water levels are high enough. Across the creek you can see where Breakneck Run enters. Soon you cross the first of many seeps. The trail climbs above the creek level only to descend again several times. At 1.0 km (0.6 mile) it turns right and climbs steeply through a hemlock grove. At 1.1 km (0.7 mile) the hardest part is over and the trail proceeds through fairly open woods, crossing a couple of side streams.

At 1.7 km (1.1 miles) the cliffs close in from the right and the trail continues along a bench. You pass above a fairly recent landslide at 2.0 km (1.3 miles), then a 1983 slide. Black birch, red maple and sumac now grow on this site.

Next, the trail descends steeply on switchbacks and crosses still another landslide (1990) at the bottom. At 3.4 km (2.1 miles) you reach Walnut Flats, a level area in the midst of the gorge. You are back at creek level.

You now enter the most remote portion of the Gorge Trail. Cross a stream and then climb to a bench above the creek. It is this bench that makes the Gorge Trail possible. You cross a series of gullies cut by side streams. The steepness of the valley walls made logging difficult to impossible so some old-growth oak, beech, hemlock, basswood and maples survive along stretches of the trail. Blowdowns are nearly a meter in diameter and are difficult to clear even with a chain saw. Sometimes the trail is simply rerouted around a blowdown. Listen to the wind in the trees and sounds of the creek below. This is the way it was two centuries ago from the lakes to the sea.

At 6.0 km (3.8 miles) you reach an unblazed but obvious side trail on the left to where Hell Run enters Slippery Rock Creek. Descend for a last view of the creek and small waterfall on Hell Run. On returning, turn up Hell Run to a side stream and cross a horse path. Beyond the stream, bear right and then turn left,

climbing to the edge of the valley above Hell Run.

Cross a natural bridge at 7.3 km (4.6 miles). Here a side stream has dissolved the limestone underneath the trail. At 7.6 km (4.7 miles) there is another natural bridge, followed shortly by a view across Hell Run, and then a hemlock glen.

Next you cross another horse path, another stream and climb still higher. Chestnut oak and mountain laurel grow here as well as wild azalea. At 8.4 km (5.2 miles) the trail skirts a corner of private land. The border is marked with white blazes. At several places it is these boundaries, rather than the lay of the land, that determines the trail route. The trail next descends, crossing a footbridge at 8.9 km (5.5 miles). The trail here shows signs of heavy use. After returning to Hell Run you cross three more bridges over seeps and side streams to reach a junction with the main but unblazed Hell's Hollow Trail. Turn right and cross Hell Run on a footbridge to the parking lot and the car you left there.

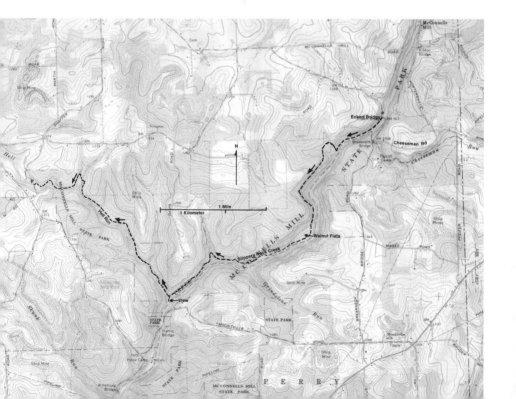

41

Enlow Fork

In-and-out distance: 10.6 km (6.6 miles)
Time: 3½ hours
Rise: 85 meters (280 feet)
Highlights: Wildflowers
Map: USGS 7½' Wind Ridge

By means of a cooperative effort involving two public agencies, a large corporation and the Western Pennsylvania Conservancy, the 405 hectare (1,000 acre) Enlow Fork Natural Area has been permanently protected as State Game Land 302. The Enlow Fork of Wheeling Creek forms the boundary between Greene and Washington counties near the West Virginia line. This hike is an easy one with special rewards for birders and all who like wildflowers. Along the Enlow Fork the ranges of southern and western plants and trees overlap the ranges of plants and trees more familiar to Pennsylvanians. The hike follows an old dirt road now closed to traffic along the bottom lands bordering the Enlow Fork. It is an in-and-out hike so it can be truncated anywhere by just retracing your footsteps.

The trailhead is deep in the hills and hollows of southwestern Pennsylvania. Take exit 2 from I-70 at Claysville and turn right (east) on US 40. After 0.9 mile turn right (south) on PA 231. Follow PA 231 for 3.5 miles and bear right where PA 231 starts downhill. Continue for 7.9 miles to a junction in West Finley and turn left. Follow this road for 2.4 miles and turn sharply right over an iron

bridge at Burdette. Follow this gravel road uphill for 1.7 miles and turn very sharply right (more than 90 degrees) onto another gravel road. A sign at this junction says State Game Land. Follow this road for 1.2 miles downhill and park in a field on your left just before you come to a gate across this road. Despite the length of this hike and some wet spots ordinary walking shoes should be adequate.

To start the hike, squeeze around the gate and follow the dirt road past the stone abutments of an old bridge across the Enlow Fork to an extensive meadow (which is an old corn field). The Game Commission management plan calls for maintaining these fields by mowing them.

At 0.7 km (0.4 mile) the old road turns sharply to the south. Look on your right for the chinquapin or yellow oak. It resembles chestnut oak but its leaves are white and hairy underneath and it rarely grows to tree size.

At 1.1 km (0.7 mile) you cross an iron bridge over Enlow Fork. Look for a giant sycamore on your left. In May you will also find hectares of blue-eyed Mary and Virginia bellflower along this part of the trail. Blue-eyed Mary is a plant of

Steel bridge over Enlow Fork

the Middle West and is rarely found in Pennsylvania.

Birds found along the Enlow Fork are indigo bunting, scarlet tanager, pileated woodpecker, downy woodpecker, belted kingfisher and yellow throated warbler.

At 2.1 km (1.3 miles) and 2.3 km (1.4 miles) roads enter from the right. In theory they are both gated off above, but on my visit this gate was broken as were two other gates farther downstream. None of these gates were capable of actually being locked. There is a giant elm tree on the left just past the second road and a stone chimney on the right.

At 2.5 km (1.6 miles) pass another iron bridge on your left and continue down the dirt road. Ruins of a log structure can be seen at 3.8 km (2.4 miles); at 4.0 km (2.5 miles) cross still another iron bridge on the deck of which there may be flood debris.

At 5.2 km (3.2 miles) you will see a flood control dam to your right. The dam has an opening at its base that allows the stream to pass through. In times of flood, the excess water is held temporarily behind the dam and only the normal flow continues downstream.

Just beyond there is another gate across the road. Turn back and retrace your steps to your car.

Other hiking opportunities in southwestern Pennsylvania are at Ryerson Station State Park (Hike 43).

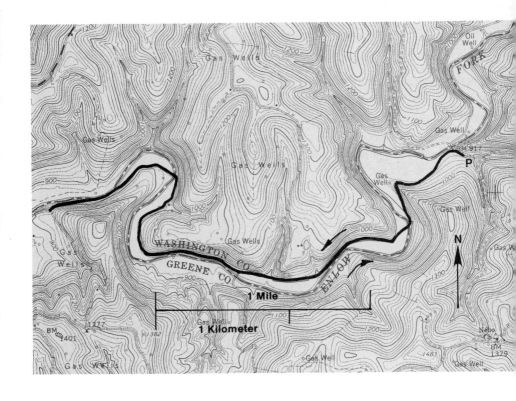

Moraine State Park

Distance: 16.2 km (10.1 miles)
Time: 5½ hours
Rise: 490 meters (1610 feet)
Highlights: Glacier Ridge Trail; Lake Arthur
Maps: USGS 7½' Prospect; state park map

Moraine State Park is located about one hour north of Pittsburgh at the junction of I-79 and US 422. Glacial Lake Arthur and Lake Edmond, just to the north, were created when the continental glacier blocked the valleys of Slippery Rock and Muddy creeks. A dam on Muddy Creek recreates Lake Arthur, although the original lake was considerably higher and some six miles longer. The terminal moraines of the Illinoian Ice Sheet and two major advances of the Wisconsin glacier are located just to the north and west of Moraine State Park. Before the park could be opened to the public, over 400 abandoned oil, gas and water wells had to be plugged to stop seepage that would have polluted the lake.

Most recreational opportunities at Moraine utilize Lake Arthur, but the roadless northern shore has an attraction for hikers on the Glacier Ridge Trail. This trail currently extends from near the west end of Lake Arthur to Jennings Environmental Education Center on PA 8. To the west, the Glacier Ridge Trail will be extended across private land to McConnells Mill State Park on Slippery Rock Creek. The Glacier Ridge Trail has been designated as part of the North Country National Scenic Trail, which is to extend over 5,000 km (3,200 miles) from Crown Point in New York to the Missouri River in North Dakota.

To reach the trail head, take exit 29 from I-79 and head east on US 422 for 5.8 miles. Then turn north on PA 528 for 4.5 miles where a road turns right to a boat launch area. Park along the west side of PA 528 near a post with a North Country Trail logo. Because of the length of this extra-vehicular activity, hiking boots are recommended.

To start this hike, cross under a power line, turn left and climb steeply up the hillside, following the faded blue blazes. After 200 meters the trail skirts a corner of private land and turns away from the power line. Continue climbing through a grove of dogwood to reach the top of the hill. At 1.2 km (0.7 mile) you pass under another power line to a junction with a yellow-blazed side trail at 1.3 km (0.8 mile). Bear right on the Glacier Ridge Trail and follow it down to the edge of Trout Cove where you turn right. To the left, the yellow-blazed Lake Shore Trail leads to the PA 528 bridge.

Lake Arthur

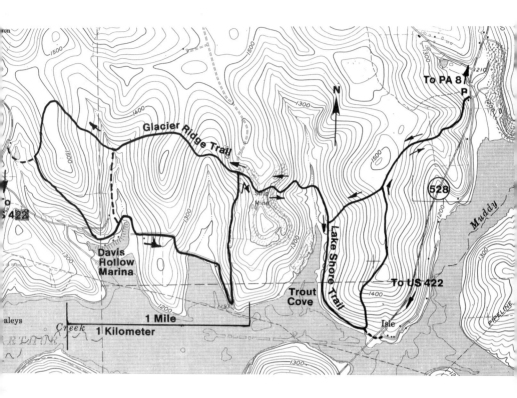

Cross a bridge over a stream at 2.6 km (1.6 miles) and climb the next ridge. At the top, enter a meadow (actually a reclaimed strip mine). Partway across bear right, paralleling a pine plantation. At the far edge of the old mine, 3.6 km (2.2 miles), cross a dirt road, reenter the woods and descend. Turn right on a woods road and ignore occasional yellow blazes. Climb over a third ridge, cross a stream on a bridge built of pressure-treated lumber and reach a trail junction at 5.4 km (3.3 miles). To the left a yellow-blazed trail leads to the Davis Hollow Marina. Turn right on the blue-blazed Glacier Ridge Trail. There are good-sized trees along this stretch, a welcome change from some of the scrubby trees near the beginning. Climb over a fourth ridge to a junction at 6.8

km (4.2 miles). Turn left on this yellow-blazed side trail and follow it downhill to Davis Hollow Marina at 7.8 km (4.8 miles). If you forgot your lunch there is a restaurant, open in summer, to the right. Keep left through the marina, avoiding a yellow-blazed hiking trail that you pass immediately. Instead, make your way to the far corner of the marina at the tip of an inlet. Walk across a bridge at the tip of the inlet and then bear right along an unmarked but mowed path along the water's edge. At 8.2 km (5.1 miles) turn left on an old road that rises out of the lake and follow it over a hill. It is marked with some orange diamonds, proclaiming it a snowmobile trail in season.

On the far side of the hill the old road divides a marsh to your left from Lake Arthur on your right. The roadway is slightly elevated so it is not wet. At 8.9 km (5.5 miles) you cross an old stone bridge. At the far side of the meadow the old road rises a bit, but continues straight along the base of a hill to a junction at 9.5 km (5.9 miles). Turn left here and follow this old road, which is also marked with an occasional orange diamond, uphill past some stone ruins on the right. At 10.7 km (6.7 miles) turn right on the Glacier Ridge Trail and retrace your steps across the old strip mine and down to Trout Cove. This time continue straight ahead on the yellow-blazed Lake Shore Trail. (You would save distance by staying on the Glacier Ridge, but you won't save any climbing.)

The Lake Shore Trail takes you past water lilies, a wood duck box and the ruins of a springhouse. (Did all the drilling and mining in this valley dry up the spring?) Turn left at 13.3 km (8.3 miles) on an old road with occasional faded yellow blazes. Climb to the top of the ridge and continue to the junction with the Glacier Ridge Trail at 14.9 km (9.3 miles). Bear right and retrace your steps down the hill to PA 528 and your car.

Additional hiking opportunities at Moraine State Park are the Glacier Ridge Trail along PA 528 (Hike 39) and the Sunken Garden and Hill Top Nature Trails near the park office, south of the lake.

Ryerson Station State Park

Distance: 8.6 km (5.3 miles)
Time: 3 hours
Rise: 240 meters (800 feet)
Highlight: Ryerson Lake
Maps: USGS 7½' Wind Ridge; state park map

Ryerson Station State Park consists of only 471 hectares (1,165 acres) on the north branch of the Dunkard Fork of Wheeling Creek in Greene County, a few kilometers from the West Virginia line. It's named after Fort Ryerson, built nearby in 1792 by order of Virginia authorities. The fort was a place of refuge for settlers during Indian raids.

Ryerson Station State Park can be reached from PA 21 about 22 miles west of I-79 or from PA 18 about nine miles from Holbrook. From PA 21 turn east on SR 3022 for 0.8 mile and then turn right, crossing the ford below the Ryerson Lake dam. Continue for 0.7 mile to the large parking area that serves the picnic area and trailhead. Ordinary walking shoes are suitable for this hike.

To the right of the map board at the trailhead move into the woods on the Fox Feather Trail and shortly turn right on the Lazear Trail. The Lazear Trail, named after a former landowner, passes through some spruce plantings. At 0.5 km (0.3 mile) you pass a "wolf tree" to the right of the trail. This white oak, thought to be 300 years old, grew wide, spreading branches that now shade out trees underneath. Thus it wolfs down the

sunlight. This eliminates the competition but doesn't produce much saw timber. "Wolf tree" is an expression used by foresters.

Soon you also pass some poison ivy. Note the furry or hairy appearance of this well-established vine, which can help you to identify poison ivy even in winter.

At 0.8 km (0.5 mile) the Orchard Trail diverges left, but you bear right, passing a shagbark hickory. The top of the hill is reached at 1.3 km (0.8 mile) and provides a view of the lake more than 120 meters below. Continuing on the Lazear Trail, you pass through a small meadow with more poison ivy before the trail descends into Mennell Hollow. Along the way you pass a sycamore "wolf tree." The Tiffany Ridge Trail diverges to the left at 2.3 km (1.4 miles). The trails on this hill are liberally provided with benches should you decide to sit down and rest or contemplate.

Shortly beyond the Tiffany Ridge Trail you pass a large white oak killed by lightning. The Tiffany Ridge Trail rejoins the Lazear Trail at 2.8 km (1.8 miles) as

Wolf Tree

WOLF TREE

OVER 300 YEARS AGO, THIS OAK TREE
WAS THE ONLY TREE GROWING IN WHAT
WAS THEN AN OPEN AREA IT RECEIVED
SUNLIGHT FROM ALL SIDES, SO IT GREW
IN ALL DIRECTIONS NOW THAT THE WOODS
HAS GROWN UP AROUND IT, IT STILL
DOMINATES THE AREA BY CREATING SHADE
WHICH PREVENTS OTHER TREES FROM
GROWING UNDER IT. HENCE THE NAME
WOLF TREE

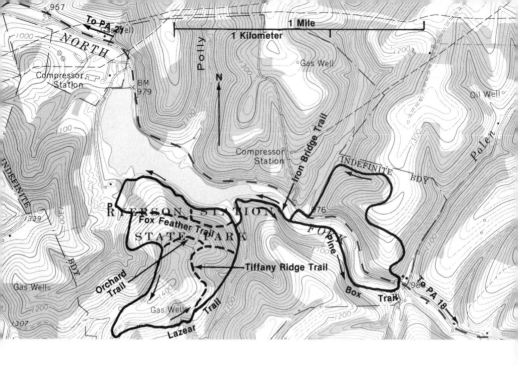

does the Fox Feather shortly beyond. At 3.1 km (1.9 miles) you turn right on the Iron Bridge Trail, cross the stream in the bottom of the hollow and soon emerge along the edge of Ryerson Lake. Occasional bass croaks from the bottom of the bank announce the presence of bullfrogs. The Iron Bridge itself is reached at 3.7 km (2.3 miles). It once served a road across the North Fork but now carries only foot traffic. You will cross it on your way back, so pass it by for now and continue on the Pine Box Trail along the water's edge. Ignore a swath to the right, and at 4.3 km (2.7 miles) climb the stream bank and shortly after, emerge into a field. At 4.7 km (2.9 miles) turn left on the road and cross a bridge over the North Fork to reach SR 3022. Cross this paved road and bear left on the Pine Box Trail. Continue up the hill to 5.3 km (3.3 miles) where the trail leads ahead to the Stahl Cemetery. Now you see the origin of the Pine Box Trail. More than 40 people came up this hill in pine boxes. Curiously, there aren't any Stahls in the Stahl Cemetery;

mostly, they are named Chess or Parson.

Back on the Pine Box Trail, you continue around the side of the hill along the contour before descending along the edge of a ravine that contains some large oak. At the bottom of Applegate Hollow you bear left and reach LR 30039 at 6.8 km (4.3 miles). Turn right, cross the Iron Bridge, retrace your route on the Iron Bridge Trail and then turn right on the Lazear Trail. At 7.8 km (4.9 miles) there is a view of the lake. Keep right and you will come out at its edge. Cross a bridge next to the lake and follow the trail cut into the hillside. This brings you to a confusing four-way trail junction at 8.1 km (5.1 miles). Turn right to return to the lake shore. Pass behind the boat rental hut and bear left through the picnic area past a drinking fountain and restrooms to the parking lot.

There are other hikes in Ryerson Station State Park on the Three Mitten, Polly Hollow, Iron Bridge and Deer trails north of the lake. Enlow Fork (Hike 41) is also in Greene County.

Schollard's Wetlands

In-and-Out Distance: 9.3 km (5.8 miles)
Time: 3 hours
Rise: 50 meters (165 feet)
Highlights: Waterfall; marsh
Maps: USGS 7½' Mercer, Harlansburg

Glaciation confuses the previous drainage of a region. Old stream valleys are filled with sand and gravel, and meltwater from the glacier may cut new valleys in new directions. The results when the glacier retreats are lakes, marshes and waterfalls. Hikers in the resulting wetlands can be certain of getting their feet wet except on this hike. The abandoned grade of the Western New York and Pennsylvania Railroad permits hikers to traverse along Schollard's Run. This is an easy, level hike with virtually no climbing and should be suitable for hikers with heart trouble.

The 485 hectares (1,200 acres) of Schollard's Wetlands were acquired by the Western Pennsylvania Conservancy in 1967 and later transferred to the Pennsylvania Game Commission. The area is designated as State Game Lands 284. The game commission uses the railroad grade as a management road, but it is gated off to ordinary traffic. The Schollard for whom the stream and wetland are named operated a blast furnace in the hollow below Springfield Falls in the 1840s.

The trailhead can be reached from exit 31 on I-79. Go west on PA 208 for 3.7 miles. Then turn south on PA 19 for 0.7 mile and bear left on a paved road.

Follow this road for 1.4 miles and then turn left on Nelson Road, which is also paved, for 0.3 mile. Park in a game commission parking lot on the right but don't block a gated road at the far end of this lot. Good walking shoes should be fine for this hike. In spring, summer and early fall, you will also need long pants, long sleeves and plenty of insect repellent.

To start this hike, turn right on Nelson Road, and after 100 meters turn left on the gated railroad grade. By 0.7 km (0.4 mile) you reach an extensive cattail marsh to your left. Soon there is open water to your right. Note the bluebird boxes affixed to the utility poles. As you move north, metal cylinders with peaked tops used as nesting boxes for wood ducks will come into view. No, there is no perch for the wood duck. The wood duck flies straight towards the hole and folds his wings at the last moment to pop into the box.

The old railroad grade divides the marsh like a dike. At 1.6 km (1.0 mile) the power line that has been following the old railroad grade diverges to the left. Farther on note a large stand of horsetails growing along the railroad grade on your right.

Plants and trees growing along the

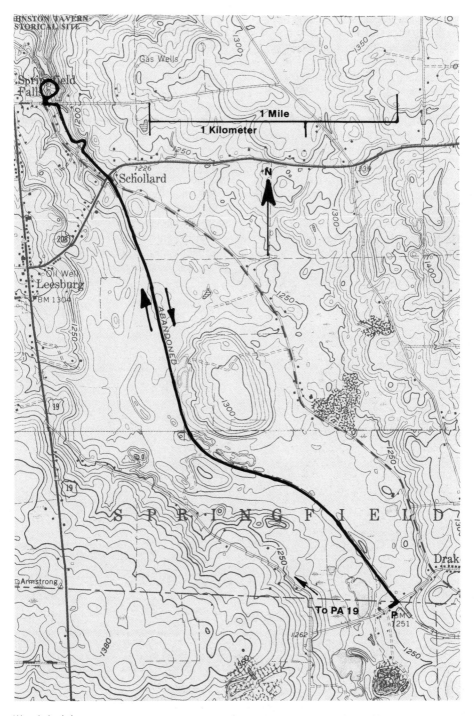

Wood duck box

way provide seeds, wild grapes and berries as food for wildlife. Among the trees are cucumber, dogwood, white oak, red maple, black cherry, elm, red oak, shingle oak and chestnut oak.

At 3.7 km (2.3 miles) cross PA 208 with care and continue on a mowed swath, which presently returns to the grade of the WNY & PRR. At 3.9 km (2.4 miles) there is a missing bridge. DO NOT try to cross the culvert pipes here as it is a long way down. Instead, bear right and make your way downstream. Here you will find rocks or even a large log on which to cross Schollard's Run. Then scramble up the side of the old railroad grade and continue to Falls Road at 4.3 km (2.7 miles).

Turn left and walk up the rise to a stop sign. Then turn right and continue past Springfield Manor (antiques for sale) and find the Springfield Falls Nature Trail just beyond. Cross the lawn and bear right into the woods. The nature trail has signs identifying trees (butternut, black cherry), shrubs (spicebush) and plants (poison ivy) along the way. At 4.6 km (2.9 miles) turn left for a view of Springfield Falls. Note the large hemlock growing in the glen below.

Return to the nature trail and turn left. Follow the nature trail back to the lawn around Springfield Manor. Turn left at the stop sign on Falls Road and retrace your steps across Schollard's Wetlands to the game commission parking lot.

Erie and the North

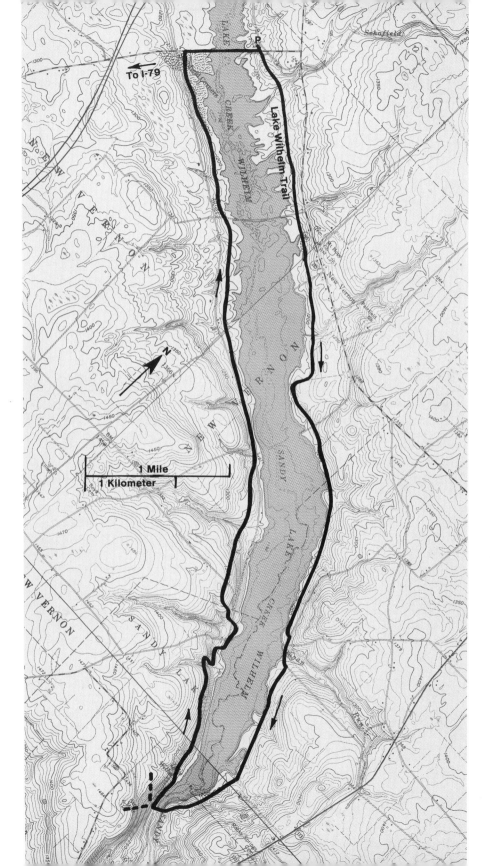

M. K. Goddard State Park

Distance: 20.6 km (12.8 miles)
Time: 7 hours
Rise: 165 meters (540 feet)
Highlight: Lake Wilhelm
Maps: USGS 7½' Sandy Lake, New Lebanon, Hadley; state
*   park map*

Maurice K. Goddard State Park, around Lake Wilhelm in Mercer County, honors a Penn State forestry professor who became head of the Pennsylvania Department of Forests and Waters in 1955. Dr. Goddard served in the cabinets of more governors than anyone else in the history of the state. When the Department of Environmental Resources was created in 1971, he became secretary and served until 1979. One ambition of Dr. Goddard's was to have a state park within 40 kilometers (25 miles) of every citizen in the Commonwealth. Lake Wilhelm is a flood control reservoir named for Lawrence J. Wilhelm, director of the Mercer County Soil and Water Conservation District and a Mercer County commissioner.

This long hike is a real bootbuster but a great deal of effort has been expended on these trails and the footway is excellent. Even the tiniest streams pass through culverts so there are scarcely any wet spots. There are no real climbs but there is a lot of gentle up-and-down. By spotting a car in the parking lot below the dam, the hike could be turned into two 10 km (6.2 miles) car shuttle hikes.

The trailhead can be reached from exit 34 on I-79. Turn west on PA 358 for 0.4 mile and then bear right on a paved road. After 1.1 miles turn right on another paved road and proceed north for 2.3 miles, passing under I-79 and over Lake Wilhelm. Then turn left into boat launch No. 3 and park there. (Park maps are available at the park office, 0.1 mile farther up the concrete road.)

Despite the length of this hike you might get away with good walking shoes due to the generally good footway, but hiking boots are preferable. Despite the absence of blazing and a shortage of trail signs, the way is usually easy to follow except when crossing fields and some other open areas. Where it crosses roads the path is usually obstructed with a single post bearing 6 yellow stripes at a 45 degree angle. Although these posts are not intended to mark the trail they are frequently useful in spotting where it exits at the far side of an open area or where it jogs across a road.

To start the hike, head back up the entrance road and cross the concrete highway with care. Pass a large sign marking the start of the Lake Wilhelm

Trail and follow the mowed path through alternating meadows and patches of woods. In the fall the meadows are filled with goldenrod. Note the bluebird houses at many points along the trail. If these houses are serviced daily to expel starlings and sparrows during the spring then there should be a bumper crop of bluebirds.

Soon the trail passes through some old stone walls. Many of the meadows are reverting to woods. Note the prevalence of small crab apples coming up amongst the goldenrod. From the meadows there are frequent views of Lake Wilhelm which fills the long narrow valley of Sandy Creek.

At 1.7 km (1.1 miles) pass a large maple tree that must have grown here when these woods were still fields. Note that the bridges on this trail have been built to accommodate the snowmobiles that use this trail in winter.

Cross a paved road at 2.2 km (1.4 miles) that leads right to boat launch area No. 4. In season there are rest rooms and drinking water at all the boat launches and the Goddard Marina. The Lake Wilhelm Trail continues through alternating woods and meadows.

At 3.2 km (2.0 miles) you reach the first challenge to your pathfinding skill in the shape of a big meadow with no mowed swath. Go straight ahead and then bear right along the edge of the woods to find where the trail continues. At 3.6 km (2.3 miles) you reach a large field. Turn sharply right along the edge of this field and continue along the lake edge and around a small patch of woods. On the far side, pick up the mowed swath where it reenters the woods.

Soon the trail emerges at another field and follows a line of trees to the left along the field edge. Continue along this same line of trees into the next field and follow it to the far corner. Here there is a snowmobile bridge over a stream and a single orange diamond by way of a marker.

At 4.8 km (3.0 miles) jog right 20 meters on an old road and then continue through a clearing, passing a low structure. Continue as before through alternating woods and meadows. At one point the trail comes very close to the lake where there is an old stone wall on the left.

At 7.3 km (4.5 miles) turn left on a gravel road and then right on a paved road. (This is the eastern limit of the use of the Lake Wilhelm Trail by snowmobiles.) Continue on the paved road across Dugan Run and turn right on the trail at 7.6 km (4.7 miles).

Continue through meadows and patches of woods; soon the dam is visible ahead. At 9.8 km (6.I miles) cross the spillway and bear right along the top of the dam. Note this is a flood control dam so the water level is well below the spillway. Pass a stairway leading down the face of the dam to a parking lot and rest rooms. At 10.0 km (6.2 miles) turn right on Creek Road, which is paved at this point. Avoid the Goddard-McKeever Trail, which is straight ahead. The park map shows a connection between the Goddard-McKeever Trail and the hiking trail to the Goddard Marina but this bit of trail was not completed in the fall of 1989.

Proceed along the paved road for 460 meters, keeping a sharp watch on the left hand side of the road. Here you will find a trail entering the woods marked by only one of the yellow striped posts. Turn left and in 20 meters turn right.

At 10.6 km (6.6 miles) cross a new pipeline swath and continue through the woods. After proceeding along the edge of the hill for another kilometer (.62 mile), the trail switchbacks down the

Lake Wilhelm

side of the hill and crosses Creek Road at 11.9 km (7.4 miles).

Bear left through boat launch area No. 1 and find the mowed trail at the far end of the parking lot. Recross Creek Road and then cross Donnelly Road. Continue in front of a garage. (The park map is in error at this point.)

Cross a stone bridge and at 12.6 km (7.8 miles) turn left and climb. There are several ways to reach the top of the hill but turn right along the field edge at the top. There is a single blue diamond marking this trail for cross-country skiing.

At the far edge of the field, swing left above a gravel road. Jog right on the gravel road for 30 meters and proceed along the edge of the woods. At 13.1 km (8.2 miles) enter the woods on a nice grade. These woods are unbroken and there are occasional picnic tables along the way.

Cross Creek Road for the last time at 14.6 km (9.0 miles) and then continue in the narrow band of parkland between Lake Wilhelm and Creek Road. Cross a dirt road and reach a parking area at 15.1 km (9.4 miles). There are occasional views of the lake and you can see the fields on the far side that you traversed earlier in the day.

At 16.0 km (10.0 miles) you reach the water pump at boat launch No. 2. Go diagonally across the parking lot and pick up the trail at the far corner. Continue through the woods. Note how all the streams are crossed on culverts. Pass through a parking area at 17.5 km (10.9 miles). A big maple is passed at 18.1 km (11.2 miles) and a big oak at 18.9 km (11.7 miles).

At 19.0 km (11.8 miles) bear left on a paved road in the Goddard Marina and follow it out to the concrete highway. Cross the highway and turn right facing traffic and follow the causeway across Lake Wilhelm. Then turn left for boat launch No. 3.

Other hiking opportunities at M. K. Goddard State Park are the Falling Run Nature Trail, to the west near I-79, and the Goddard McKeever Trail, back at the dam.

Presque Isle State Park

Distance: 6.3 km (3.9 miles)
Time: 2 hours
Rise: 3 meters (10 feet)
Highlights: Lake Erie; lighthouse
Maps: USGS 7½' Erie North; state park map

Presque Isle is a sand spit in the shallow waters of Lake Erie. To our eyes, it is part of the permanent landscape. But if we could take time-lapse photographs over a few hundred years, we would see it is actually moving. Beaches on the western side are washed away, only to become new land on the eastern side. Under the action of wind and waves, the entire pile of sand has moved east about 800 meters in the past century. Coming from the mainland, you pass through several centuries of plant succession. First are oak, sugar maple and hemlock—the climax vegetation. Then there are white pine, poplar, red maple and cedar—sun-loving trees that provide shade for the shade-tolerant species that form the climax forest. Next, you leave the trees behind and reach an area covered with shrubs and other small plants. Finally, at the eastern tip, you come to an area where dunes and beaches have just been formed. This new land is stabilized by young poplars whose roots anchor the moving sand.

Presque Isle has its share of human history as well. Commodore Perry's fleet was built here during the War of 1812. After defeating the British, Perry's flotilla remained at Misery Bay for the rest of the war. A full-sized replica of Perry's flagship, the "Niagara," is on display in downtown Erie.

To reach the park and trailhead from I-79, turn west on US 20 (26th Street), and then turn north on PA 832 (Peninsula Drive), which takes you out onto Presque Isle. At 1.5 miles beyond the park office, turn left and then right on Mill Road. Another 0.6 mile brings you to the trailhead for the Sidewalk Trail. Park along the road and head down the Sidewalk Trail. Ordinary walking shoes or sneakers are fine for this hike, but you will need some strong insect repellent. There is some poison ivy along the trail, but it is easily avoided. Presque Isle has also been a hot spot for Lyme disease because of its overabundant and thus heavily parasitized deer herd. A special deer hunting season in December 1989 should reduce the herd and also the danger of Lyme disease.

Pass the end of the unsigned Dead Pond Trail, which comes in from the left, and then the Marsh Trail that diverges to the right. Trees growing along this section are red oak, red maple, chokecherry, pin oak, ash and willow. The Sidewalk Trail was once a nature trail and some of the numbered posts still survive. However, the trail guide is no longer available.

Lake Erie

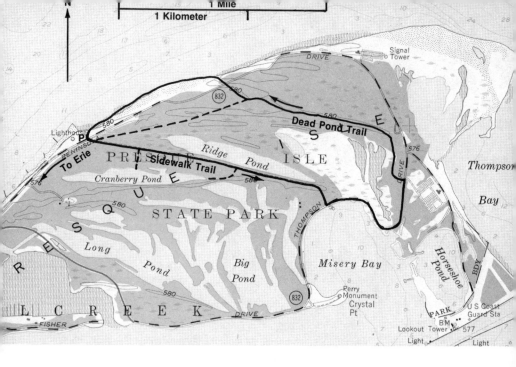

At 1.0 km (0.6 mile) the Fox Trail veers right, and soon you can see the open water of Ridge Pond to your left. The pond is a good habitat for ducks, and you may be able to hear them, even if you can't see them. Serviceberry and chokecherry grow along this section. Both fruits are edible. The serviceberry when fresh is delicious; chokecherries are extremely tart and really pucker up your mouth.

Soon the Sidewalk Trail turns right and ends at Thompson Road on the edge of Misery Bay where Perry's fleet was stationed. The Perry Monument can be seen across the bay. Turn left along Thompson Drive and keep left, facing traffic, as you round the edge of Niagara Pond. Poplars grow along the bay and on the far side of the pond there are gray birch and pitch pine.

At 3.1 km (1.9 miles) turn left onto the unsigned Bush Trail, opposite a road on the right. Deer tracks show that people are not the only ones using the trails. Soon you turn left on the unsigned Dead Pond Trail. Like the Sidewalk Trail, this trail is mostly in the open, but whenever you pass through a patch of woods, the deer flies close in. Most insect repellents don't seem to bother deer flies.

At 4.6 km (2.9 miles) bear right at a fork in the trail. This is the B Trail, and it soon brings you out to the Pine Tree Road. Cross the road, proceed to the beach, and bear left. Lake Erie is truly an inland sea. You can't see the other side. Erie and the other great lakes are the world's largest deposits of fresh water in the liquid state.

Continue along the beach until you approach the lighthouse. The lighthouse isn't very high and just barely gets above the tree tops. This is your landmark to turn inland, and you should come out on the road within sight of your car.

A paved trail that has been built along the bay side from the park entrance to Perry's monument presents another hiking opportunity at Presque Isle State Park.

Erie Extension Canal Towpath

In-and-out distance: 9.6 km (6.0 miles)
Time: 3 hours
Rise: 3 meters (10 feet)
Highlights: Pymatuning Swamp; waterfowl
Maps: USGS 7½' Conneaut Lake, Hartstown; Sportsman's
Recreation map—State Game Lands No. 214

In the 1830s and 1840s, Pennsylvania underwent a vast program of canal building. By the 1840s, canals stretched from the Delaware River to Lake Erie. These canals were not all built to the same standards. Locks on different canals were of different lengths and widths. Two rail links, the Columbia to Philadelphia Railroad in the east and the Allegheny Portage Railroad in the west, were also included. A great deal of loading and unloading was required, making the canal system uncompetitive with the fast-developing railroads. By the 1850s, the railroads had gained the upper hand. While some canals continued in use until the twentieth century, most were abandoned in the nineteenth. Most of the abandoned canals were bought by the very railroads with which they had competed. Some were destroyed in the construction of railroads and highways, others by a century of floods and the growth of trees and other vegetation. Very few old canals are now found on public lands.

One part of the Erie Extension Canal and its towpath came into public ownership by accident, with the development of adjacent Pymatuning State Park. The Erie Extension Canal originally ran from the Ohio River up Beaver Valley to Erie, with a side canal down French Creek to the Allegheny River at Franklin. It was completed in 1844. The canal crossed the backwaters of Pymatuning Swamp. As the land was flat, no locks were required.

The canal towpath across the eastern arm of Pymatuning cut off a 240 hectare (595 acre) lake, which served as a reservoir for the canal. Canals used water every time a boat went through a lock. The old canals probably lost a good deal of water through leakage as well. If a canal ran out of water, the first boat to run aground blocked the channel and halted traffic in both directions.

The old towpath makes a very different sort of hike. There is no problem in following it. And while most trails require people to walk single file, this one is wide enough for two people to walk side by side. It's a good trail for a long talk with a friend. There is a considerable amount of illegal use by all terrain vehicles.

There are a great many birds along the trail. Chickadees chatter from the trees, herons stalk the shallows, kingfishers dart into the water and a great honking over the swamp heralds the ap-

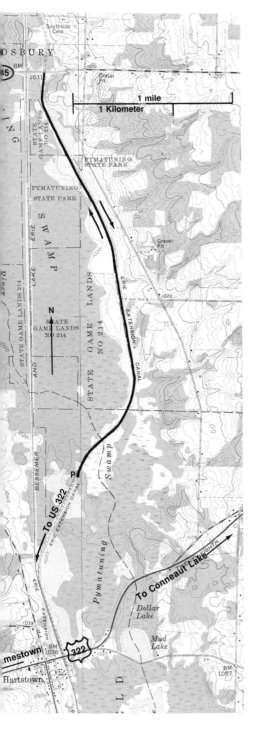

proach of a flight of geese. Don't forget your binoculars.

Although I expected the insects to be a real problem, the hike is mostly out in the open and I didn't have to use repellent, even on a warm day in July. Almost any sort of shoes should be adequate for the excellent footway on this hike.

The trailhead is reached from US 322, 5.0 miles west of the junction with PA 18 in Conneaut Lake and just east of Hartstown. Turn north at the east side of the overpass which crosses the Bessemer and Lake Erie Railroad. This gravel road is very rough at first, so take it slowly and thread your way around the mud puddles at the bottom of the slope. Turn right at the bottom and continue. The cinder road swings away from the railroad, and at 1.0 mile from US 322 you reach a gate and the game commission parking lot.

To start the hike, dodge around the gate and head out along the old towpath. Note the difference in water levels on the two sides of the towpath. The water on the right is almost two meters higher than the water on the left.

Trees along your route are chokecherry, aspen, red maple, elm, cucumber, cottonwood, walnut, locust, red oak, white oak, hickory, sassafras, willow and apple. Sumac also grows here as does wild strawberry and poison ivy. The game commission mows the route, however, so the poison ivy does not reach the path.

At 0.8 km (0.5 mile) cross a bridge over the dam that controls the level of the old reservoir. Here you see the difference in water levels clearly. This is a favorite spot for fishing. In the reservoir water lilies abound, but on the other side the ground alternates between marsh and woods. Look for deer tracks on the path. When I turned around

Open Water in the Old Canal Reservoir

once, I found a doe following me.

At 2.4 km (1.5 miles) you reach the site of an old bridge across the canal. A couple of planks across the trickle provide access for fishing. At 2.9 km (1.8 miles) farms are visible along the far side of the valley, and at 4.8 km (3.0 miles) you reach the vehicle gate next to PA 285. Along the way you have crossed an unmarked corner of Pymatuning State Park. Ahead, the old towpath continues across private land before returning to the route of the Bessemer and Lake Erie Railroad. Turn and retrace your steps along the towpath to your car.

Petroleum Center

Distance: 11.5 km (7.1 miles)
Time: 4¼ hours
Rise: 325 meters (1,070 feet)
Highlights: Waterfall; ghost town
Maps: USGS 7½' Titusville South; park map

Petroleum Center may not be the largest of Pennsylvania's ghost towns but it was certainly one of the wickedest. It was named because it was in the center of the original oil region in the 1860s, halfway between Titusville and Oil City. Within 20 years the oil boom had moved on and Petroleum Center was on its way to being a ghost town, but it had a lively time in between. President U. S. Grant visited it in 1871, and on ordinary days, a riot, fire or shooting could happen at any minute. There were shouts of new oil strikes, gushers, wild card games and brawls, all covered with mud and oil.

This circuit hike visits Petroleum Center and other oil age sites along the Oil Creek Hiking Trail, built by Ray Gerard of Titusville. The hike is entirely within the boundaries of Oil Creek State Park, which is one of five state parks established through the efforts of the Western Pennsylvania Conservancy.

The trailhead is at the headquarters for Oil Creek State Park. Drive up PA 8 and take the Oil City bypass. Then 1 mile beyond Rouseville turn right immediately after the PA 8 bridge over Oil Creek. Pass the ice control structure in the creek, and after 3.0 miles turn right

and cross Oil Creek on a steel bridge. After another 0.3 mile turn left for the parking lot at the park office. Because of many rocks and wet spots you will want your boots for this hike.

The start of the hike is marked by a Hiking Trail sign to the right of the park office. Head into the woods along the white blazes. Just after crossing a poleline you reach the junction with the yellow-blazed main Oil Creek Trail at 0.5 km (0.3 mile). Turn left and continue climbing among large boulders, recrossing the poleline.

At the top of the climb you reach the edge of Oil Creek Valley. The trail divides the hemlocks growing on the slope to your left and the deciduous trees growing on the level to your right.

A blue-blazed cross-country ski trail comes in from the right at 1.4 km (0.9 mile) and continues along the Oil Creek Trail. Soon the damage caused by the tornadoes that struck Western Pennsylvania on 31 May 1985 becomes apparent. At first there is only an occasional uprooted tree but soon you cross a swath of destroyed timber. Back on the valley edge, you can see more tornado damage on the left, which has been partially salvaged.

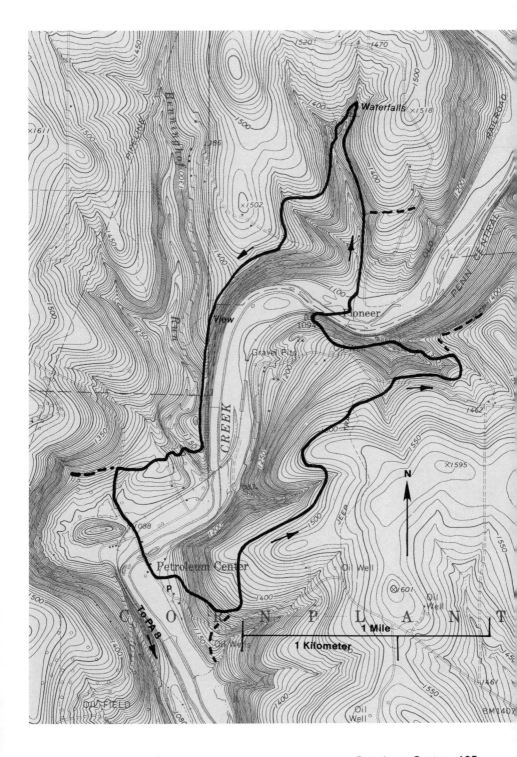

Waterfalls ×1518

×1611

PIPELINE

Hemlock Run

×1502

1985

1502

1520

1470

1500

1400

1470

PLAIN CENTRAL RAILROAD

View

Pioneer

1092

Gravel Pits

CREEK

1088

1083

1200

1200

1250

1500

JEEP

×1595

N

×1601

Petroleum Center

P

To PA 8

Oil Wells

OIL FIELD

C O R N P L A N T

1 Mile

1 Kilometer

1400

Oil Well

Oil Well

Oil Well

BM 1407

1462

1550

1550

1461

There is a trailside shelter at a trail junction at 2.8 km (1.8 miles). Bear left on the Big Loop and let the Downhill Thrill go do its own thing. The trail descends and you cross a power line. Cross Hemlock Road at 3.2 km (2.0 miles).

After crossing the headwaters of Hemlock Run and passing through some ruins, turn left on a white-blazed connector trail at 4.2 km (2.6 miles). Descend above Hemlock Run, first on a nice old grade and then on a trail next to a small pipeline. Cross Hemlock Run on some slippery rocks and then climb steeply.

At the top, pass along the very edge of a steep drop to the Oil Creek and Titusville Railroad. Descend and cross the OC and TRR at 5.3 km (3.3 miles); then bear right on the paved bicycle trail and cross Oil Creek. Note that this bridge is built on the piers of a former railroad bridge. Immediately on the far side, bear left on the connector trail.

At 5.8 km (3.6 miles) there is a trail on the right leading to a parking lot at the end of Pioneer Road. Bear left and start the climb along Pioneer Run to the West Side Trail at 6.2 km (3.8 miles) and continue climbing gently along the yellow blazes. Cross another poleline and then descend to Greg Falls at 6.8 km (4.2 miles). This is a very pretty spot and a good spot for a break.

Back on the trail, cross Pioneer Run and then double back on the far side. Descending, cross Pioneer Run two more times where a tributary comes in and climb to an old grade which passes a shack dating from the oil boom days.

At 8.2 km (5.1 miles) turn left off an old road towards a metal shack which housed another old oil well. There is a view to the left across Oil Creek at 8.6 km (5.3 miles) where the trail crosses a power line. You can see the cut made to salvage timber felled in the tornadoes of 31 May 1985.

Turn left off an old road and proceed down a ridge between Benninghof Run and Oil Creek. Soon the trail enters an area of tornado damage and continues on a logging road, passing another view of Oil Creek. At 10.2 km (6.3 miles) cross Benninghof Run and a paved road.

Continue through open woods and old fields, passing many ruins of the petroleum age.

At 10.8 km (6.7 miles) turn left on a dirt road, which is actually the connector trail through Petroleum Center. Cross the Oil City and Titusville Railroad at the new depot and enter downtown Petroleum Center. There are many interpretive signs along the walking tour. At the center of town only the stone steps of the bank remain.

To complete the hike, walk across the steel bridge (one lane wide but two-way traffic) and make your way to the park office and its parking lot.

Other hiking opportunities at Oil Creek State Park include a circuit hike based at Drake Well Historic Site (Hike 50). Other circuit hikes could be made by using the PA 8 bridge, downstream, or from the Miller Farm Historic Site, upstream.

Oil Creek Trail

Allegheny Gorge

Distance: 11.7 km (7.3 miles)
Time: 3¾ hours
Rise: 310 meters (1,020 feet)
Highlights: Old iron furnace; view; mountain stream
Maps: USGS 7½' Kennerdell; state forest trail map for
  Allegheny Tract

In the 1970s the state purchased 1,280 hectares (3,160 acres) along the Allegheny River in Venango County for a new state park to be called Allegheny Gorge. The tract included some ten kilometers along the Allegheny River where it has cut a canyon, more than 150 meters deep, through the plateau. The land had been heavily used in the past, first for subsistence farming, then for charcoal iron manufacturing and, more recently, for gas and oil drilling. Funds to develop the new park did not materialize, and the land became part of Kittanning (alias Clear Creek) State Forest. With an adjoining tract of State Game Lands 39, the area is more than 1,600 hectares (4,000 acres). Cooperation between the Bureau of Forestry and the Grove City College Outing Club is producing a network of hiking trails and cross-country ski trails above and along the Allegheny River. One impressive overlook has been cleared and another is planned.

Allegheny Gorge is most easily reached from new PA 8. Exit at PA 308 and turn northwest toward Pearl. Turn right on old PA 8 for 0.4 mile and then turn right on Dennison Run Road (T-368). Continue east for 1.7 miles and then turn right on T-371 for 1.1 miles to a game commission parking lot at the end of the road. Hiking boots or good walking shoes should be fine for this hike.

To start, head south from the parking lot along the gated game commission management road. The game commission has permitted trail signs to be posted. At 0.4 km (0.3 mile) bear left on an old road that leads into the woods. Old earthworks are encountered at 1.2 km (0.8 mile). They are thought to be bog iron pits, which provided iron ore for several local furnaces. The pits can be followed for long distances at this elevation as they followed the outcrop of ore.

Cross the boundary of state forest land at 1.4 km (0.9 mile). From here on, the trail is marked with orange paint blazes. Turn right for Bullion Run Iron Furnace; you will return on one of the other blazed trails at this junction.

View of Allegheny River

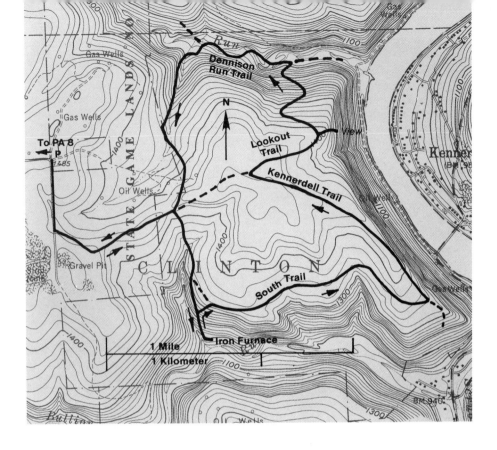

Continue past a spring to the right of the trail, and then cross a bridge over a small stream in a hemlock grove. Bear right at 1.9 km (1.2 miles) for the iron furnace. The trail follows an old road down a tributary of Bullion Run. Unlike other parts of the state, here charcoal was made at the furnace rather than out in the woods. This road was used to bring the necessary iron ore and wood. Apparently the lure of hauling wood to the furnace was too much for the farmers. Subsistence farming collapsed in favor of a cash economy. Turn left above Bullion Run Iron Furnace for a view of the stack that has been cleared and a sign providing information on the operation of the furnace. The furnace was built in 1840 and operated for only ten years. Only eight or nine men were

employed in its operation. It consumed 100 acres of woodland per year for charcoal even though it shut down over the summer. It could produce 3 tons of iron per day. The pig iron was hauled to the Allegheny River for shipment to Pittsburgh aboard white pine rafts that floated down from Tionesta every spring.

After you've seen the furnace, climb back up the trail through the hemlock grove and bear right at 2.9 km (1.8 miles) on a trail to Kennerdell. Bear right again at the trail junction at the top of the hill. This trail takes you through open woods at the edge of the plateau above Bullion Run, and presently you see ruins of old oil wells. The metal rods crossing the trail indicate that a central engine was used to pump a number of wells simultaneously. It's said a steam engine was used to pump these wells, which would make this installation older than the Olin Natural gas engine on display at the Drake Well Museum near Titusville.

At 5.0 km (3.1 miles) turn left on the Kennerdell Road. The trail sign identifies it only as a cross-country ski trail. It is also orange-blazed and goes along the edge of the plateau above the Allegheny River. Note an oil pipeline of small diameter which soon crosses the road and then parallels it. At 6.1 km (3.8 miles) a woods road comes in from the left. Turn right at 6.5 km (4.1 miles) on the Lookout Trail to reach the Dennison Point overlook. This trail is marked with faded blue blazes.

The overlook is a good 120 meters above the Allegheny. Part of the village of Kennerdell can be seen across the river and you can also see far up river.

At this point you could truncate the hike by retracing your steps and turning right on the Kennerdell Trail, but a great deal of time and money has been expended in building four suspension bridges across Dennison Run which make the extended hike worthwhile.

Just in back of the overlook turn on the orange-blazed Dennison Run Trail and follow it down an eroded old road to the stream. At 8.2 km (5.1 miles) turn left upstream and cross the first of the suspension bridges. Continue upstream across two more suspension bridges to a trail junction at 8.9 km (5.5 miles).

Turn left at a sign for the Bullion Run Iron Furnace and cross the fourth suspension bridge. Continue upstream, crossing a bridge over a side stream. Then turn left, climb steeply, passing cascades and small waterfalls. Near the top, cross a bridge over the stream and continue past an old oil or gas well.

Turn right on a woods road at 10.0 km (6.3 miles) and cross a corner of State Game Lands 39. In just 200 more meters you reach the major trail junction with the Iron Furnace and Kennerdell trails. Bear right and retrace your steps to the game lands parking lot.

There are additional hiking opportunities here in the Allegheny River Tract. The Pipeline and Ridge trails make a loop to the north of Dennison Run. Access to these trails is provided by two parking lots along T-368. The state forest map will suggest other loops.

50

Oil Creek State Park

Distance: 8.5 km (5.3 miles)
Time: 3 hours
Rise: 290 meters (950 feet)
Highlights: Oil Creek Gorge
Maps: USGS 7½' Titusville South; park map

This hike takes you along historic and beautiful Oil Creek, south of Titusville. Oil seeps have occurred in this valley since prehistoric times. Indians dug pits to collect the oil. Here in 1859, "Colonel" Edwin Drake drilled the world's first oil well. By good fortune, Drake struck oil only 23 meters down. Most of the producing oil sand was 150 meters below the valley floor. But Drake's luck deserted him, and he died poor, while others made fortunes along Oil Creek and at the ghost town of Pithole, just to the east. Some wells still produce oil nearby, and one has produced continuously since 1861. Pennsylvania rocks hold onto their oil so tenaciously that some of the last producing wells on dry land may turn out to be not too far from here.

The oil boom of the 1860s produced much of the technology still in use today. From the North Slope of Alaska to the floor of the North Sea to the far reaches of Siberia, inventions made here in Pennsylvania are still in use.

Much of this historic region is now contained in Oil Creek State Park, which stretches from PA 8 north to the Drake Well Historic Site. Ironically, perhaps, two attractions of this park which com-

memorate the dawn of the Petroleum Age are a bicycle trail, between the Drake Well and the park headquarters, and the Oil Creek Hiking Trail.

The Oil Creek Hiking Trail makes a loop of about 58 kilometers (36 miles), crossing Oil Creek at the ghost town of Petroleum Center and on the road bridge at the Drake Oil Well Historic Site. The trail has in large part been the retirement project of Ray Gerard of Titusville. Two overnight shelter areas have been built along the trail, permitting backpacks of up to three days. This hike makes a circuit on the most northern part of the Oil Creek Trail, using a footbridge over Oil Creek paid for by the Western Pennsylvania Conservancy. The Oil Creek Trail is one of the best maintained trails in the state. I did not find a blowdown anywhere, and at two places I saw where this year's summer growth had been trimmed.

To reach the trailhead from US 8 in Titusville, turn east at the first stoplight on the south side of town and follow Bloss Street 1.0 mile to a parking lot next to Oil Creek. This parking lot also serves the bicycle trail, so it could be crowded.

To start your hike on the yellow-

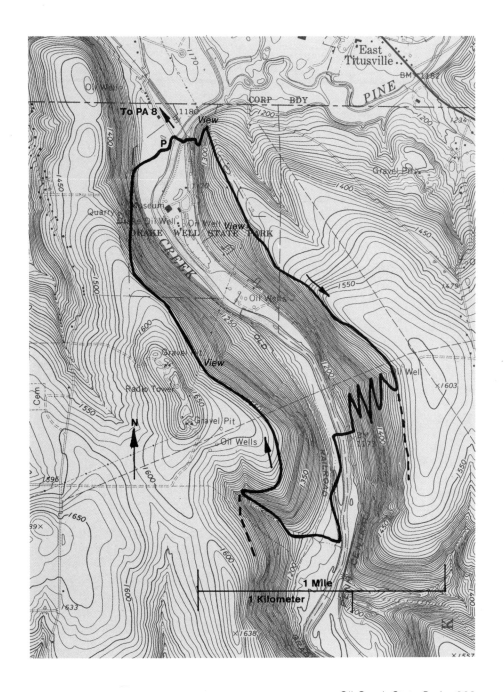

Suspension bridge over Oil Creek

blazed Oil Creek Trail, walk across Oil Creek on the one lane (two-way traffic) bridge to the Drake Well Historic Site. Then cross the railroad tracks. Beware, the Oil Creek and Titusville Railroad operates excursion trains on this line from March through October. Turn right and start to climb. Shortly, you switchback to the left on an old road to Pithole. (Pithole is Pennsylvania's largest ghost town.) At the next right turn there is a view of Titusville from a powerline swath, which will provide you with two more views farther along this hike. Pass a trail register, where you should sign in, and then cross the powerline at 1.3 km (0.8 mile). This time you get a view across Oil Creek valley.

Beyond the swath, you continue climbing through an area that burned in 1982 due to a mismanaged trash fire. At 1.7 km (1.1 miles) ignore the line of yellow blazes and white blazes crossing the trail. These appear to be the boundaries of the Drake Well Historic Site and Oil Creek Park, respectively.

Note the many sassafras seedlings growing along the trail. Sassafras leaves look like mittens. Some have left thumbs, some have right thumbs, some have thumbs on both sides, and some have none at all. Sassafras leaves are highly variable and all shapes may be found on the same tree.

Cross an old pipeline swath at 2.7 km (1.7 miles) and bear right on a white-blazed connector trail. The connector trail switchbacks down the side of Oil Creek Gorge on a set of well-preserved old road grades. At 3.7 km (2.3 miles) cross the Oil City and Titusville Railroad tracks again and then the swinging bridge over Oil Creek that makes this hike possible. At the far side, turn left (downstream) at the edge of Oil Creek. Several old apple trees suggest this was an orchard at one time.

The trail continues downstream on several old road grades, but at 4.5 km (2.8 miles) you turn right on a trail, passing an old wooden oil tank. Cross the paved bicycle trail, which follows an abandoned railroad grade and continue across a clearing containing some ruins marking the historic site of Boughton.

Continue climbing along a tiny run to 5.1 km (3.2 miles) where you turn right on the yellow-blazed West Side Trail. Switchback to the top of the hill and cross an old pipeline swath at 6.0 km (3.7 miles). Farther on, cross a two-log bridge. Note how the wire rope used as a hand rail has been grown over by the beech trees.

At 6.6 km (4.1 miles) cross the powerline for a last view across Oil Creek.

Soon the trail starts a gentle descent, passing oak trees over a meter in diameter. At 7.7 km (4.8 miles) pass another trail register. Be sure to sign in again. About 200 meters farther, turn right, cross the paved bicycle path and descend steeply on steps. At the bottom there is a bog bridge and an old steel oil tank. Note old pipes in the trail as you cross this bottom land. Soon you reach the edge of Oil Creek and head upstream to the parking lot.

There are plenty of additional hiking opportunities near Oil Creek State Park. Hike 48 in this book is a circuit hike starting from the park headquarters at Petroleum Center. A flyer from the Western Pennsylvania Conservancy describes a 20 km (12.4 miles) 2-day backpack using the Drake Well trailhead. There is a 10 km (6.2 miles) circuit hike at Two Mile Run County Park near PA 417 north of Franklin.